ROADRUNNER

SINGLES ▲ A SERIES EDITED BY JOSHUA CLOVER AND EMILY J. LORDI

Jonathan Richman around 1972, with Modern Lovers. Department of Special Collections and University Archives, W. E. B. Du Bois Library, University of Massachusetts, Amherst.

ROADRUNNER

JOSHUA CLOVER

DUKE UNIVERSITY PRESS   DURHAM AND LONDON   2021

Designed by Matthew Tauch

Typeset in Bitter and Work Sans by Copperline Book Services

Library of Congress Cataloging-in-Publication Data

Names: Clover, Joshua, author.

Title: Roadrunner / Joshua Clover.

Other titles: Singles (Duke University Press)

Description: Durham : Duke University Press, 2021. | Series:
Singles | Includes bibliographical references and index.

Identifiers: LCCN 2020049234 (print)

LCCN 2020049235 (ebook)

ISBN 9781478013471 (hardcover)

ISBN 9781478014393 (paperback)

ISBN 9781478021698 (ebook)

Subjects: LCSH: Richman, Jonathan (Vocalist)—Criticism and
interpretation. | Richman, Jonathan (Vocalist). Roadrunner
(Song) | Modern Lovers (Musical group) | Rock music—United
States—History and criticism. | Popular music—United States—
History and criticism. | Automobiles—Songs and music—History
and criticism. | Automobiles—Social aspects—United States.

Classification: LCC ML420.R5572 C56 2021 (print) |
LCC ML420.R5572 (ebook) | DDC 782.42166092—dc23

LC record available at https://lccn.loc.gov/2020049234

LC ebook record available at https://lccn.loc.gov/2020049235

CONTENTS

▶ 01 Rock & Roll Radio, 1980

THEY WERE JUST ANOTHER BAND out of Boston. Private Lightning were local heroes at the end of the seventies who got their shot at the big time with their 1980 major label debut, self-titled as unwritten law demands. They were just another band out of Boston but there were worse starting positions right around then. The Cars' self-titled debut from 1978 would move six million copies. Boston's self-titled debut from 1976 is presently the twelfth best-selling album of all time. Private Lightning never broke nationally. Perhaps it is obvious why.

"Christopher Sky is the afternoon DJ on rock & roll radio," begins "Song of the Kite," one of their lead singles. No one but Prince could get away with that name for a character in a song. Reader, I do not want to mention this but I feel compelled to note that the opening line is perfect dactylic hexameter, the verse meter of epic poetry. *The Iliad, The Aeneid, Metamorphoses*. It is almost never used in English. Adam Sherman hits the weighted syllables in "*rock & roll*" and "*radio*" fervently because those things are what matters. Rock & roll is the epic now, meaning then. Or maybe it was already lost as the epic is lost. "Do you remember rock & roll radio?" asked the Ramones in the spring of 1980, possibly on the same channel that would play "Song of the Kite" later in the set, second line of "Kite" again tracing epic meter but more loosely: "His voice is like velvet, everyone knows he was born for the studio." No one could get away with that hackneyed simile. The story develops quickly. One day while Christopher is lying in a field, he sees a beautiful kite, which rhymes with "beautiful sight" and "vision of light." He hears in his heart "an unforgettable song." This is the song of kite, the song within the song. The vision leaves him mute for seven months during which he vanishes from the airwaves and everywhere else, finally returning amid great rumor and excitation. Everybody listens in. But he does not speak, does not play recorded music in the darkened studio, "the turntables still and the tape players off." Instead he gives voice to a single song, his rendition of the song he heard that day, the song of the kite, the song that we too get to hear for the first time. Hold onto that, it bears repeating as it will repeat throughout, we are listening to the radio where someone is listening to the radio. Christopher Sky, voiced by Sherman, sings, "There is love in the world," and then he sings it again and then again. Chorus, cut.

There is no stripping away the allegory from the kite, "the color of crimson, the crossbar of wood, a tail a mile or more long." We get it. Even though the character is named Christopher, which means the exact same thing here as when Prince gave his characters and sometimes himself that name, it is the kite itself that is Christ upon the old wooden cross; the tail is the blood, the absolute and endless mark of the crucifixion across the sky of history (Elias Canetti memorably describes Christianity as "an infinite dilution of lament, spread so evenly over the centuries that scarcely anything remains of the suddenness of death and the violence of grief"[1]). Christopher's vision is followed by seven months in hell or in the desert or on the road to Damascus, the double exile that features regularly in redemption songs, both an exterior exile from society and an interior exile into ascesis, into ascetic silence and contemplation, all the saints and the lesser Christs, everyone does it and you know the drill, they eventually return from exile with a message of love. There is love in the world there is love in the world there is love in the world there is love.

It would be something if this anagogic disaster were the only Private Lightning song remembered outside the band's family members. But "Song of the Kite" was only half of a double A-side single. The track on the flip side is called "Physical Speed." This song is also interested in the radio but in a more secular register. It sounds a bit more like the Cars and it is about driving. "Physical Speed" is Private Lightning's biggest hit and it begins, "My heart is in neutral, this motionless summer." As night falls, our narrator makes the only possible move to escape his restless boredom: "I tune in my AM radio, I turn the key and I go." There's the radio.

That's the pre-chorus; then the chorus: "and I ride, and I ride, physical speed is just what I need, and I ride, and I ride, what can I do, I'm so lonely for you." The second verse circles back, repeats the scene: "out on the highway, the radio's blasting, the engine is racing, as fast as it goes." The song is not a particularly innovative retelling of rock mythology, of its old building blocks, but it is admirably efficient at setting all the elements in place and in motion within about ninety seconds: *car, highway, aimless circularity, loneliness, nighttime, rock & roll radio*. Get it, got it, go.

I have omitted one obscure detail. In the first verse, before he launches himself onto the road, our nameless driver has been busying himself otherwise: "I write all these letters to drop in the mail." We never find out to whom. Out on the highway during the second verse, a descant repeats much of the first verse in the background, with a small change: "I write *you* these letters to drop in the mail." He is driving around, the song intimates, to post a message or perhaps to hand-deliver one. But this never happens, he just rides. Nothing is delivered . . . unless the song itself is the letter he has written, the letter that someone will hear coming out of the darkness, out of the radio, the message that you will one day receive.

This leads back around to "Song of the Kite," before we leave Private Lightning behind for good, they were just here to set us in motion toward the song in the title of this book. There is another reading of the song. This reading is barely allegorical at all. It's just . . . the story. It is also an old story, a different one but one that can be combined with the story of physical speed—and is not snapping together old stories our way of being new? Is not the multiple the origin of the single? And it is this that will yield what I am going to call the ur-story, a folktale, shared and social, different in different moments, the song that is ten thousand songs.

This book is about all of them and one in particular.

The story is this: There is a fan of such enthusiasm that their life is devoted to the music of others; they are, not to be overly technical, *adjacent to the radio*. One day they encounter an ordinary object. It could be a kite but it could just as well be a neon sign or a chewing gum wrapper, we could call this object common or trivial or proletarian, *popular* in the old sense, *of the people*, but in any regard the object is a commodity because that's the fate of objects in the modern world, to be commodities and then to be their remnants, and anyway this person, this lover and curator of others' music, sees that this object is not abject and degraded but rather that it is beautiful even if it is trivial, or beautiful because it is trivial, that the world is in fact filled with such beautiful things, that the world comprises these things and is thus itself beautiful, and they need to tell you about this, they need to drive around the world to deliver their message about the extraordinariness of the ordinary, about how they are in love with the modern world. They put all of this into a song, their own song for once, they put it into a pop song because that is the disposable commodity to measure all other disposable commodities, the pure thing, the paradigm for the kite or the neon sign or the chewing gum wrapper, and although they have the radio on, or because they have the radio on, they begin to sing.

It is the most ordinary single of all time.

►02 Faster Miles an Hour, 1972

WE BEGIN ON ROUTE 128 when it's late at night. That's where the Modern Lovers begin, and the greatest song of all time, or maybe it is the greatest rock song of all time, or the greatest American rock song of all time, or the greatest American rock song of that era. I offer those specifications not to diminish the claim but because "American" and "rock" matter to the song and to this book, and "that era" matters especially, the era around 1970 when "Roadrunner" was written by a teenager named Jonathan Richman, the era around 1972 when he and his band recorded one of the best-known versions of "Roadrunner" with John Cale producing, around 1974 when the other best-known version was recorded with King Kaufman, around 1976 when the earlier version finally appeared on the Modern Lovers' self-titled debut, around 1977 when both appeared together on a single so that we could finally have a seven-inch canon, Kaufman's take on the A-side credited to Jonathan Richman and now known as "Roadrunner (Once)" even though it was recorded later, and Cale's take on the B-side credited to Modern Lovers and now known as "Roadrunner (Twice)" even though it was recorded earlier. So, around then. As always, time is out of joint.

Route 128 is Boston's inner beltway, a kind of artificial boundary to the basin around Massachusetts Bay now thought of as the greater Boston area, the traditional home of the indigenous Massachusett people and sometime later, after the delivery by settlers of epidemic, prayer, and slaughter, the home of Jonathan Richman and the Modern Lovers. Such roads are less common in the United States than in Europe, Asia, South America. They tend to encircle dense cities of the older style, giving them a sense of order, of boundedness, or at least the promise that one might circumnavigate their labyrinthine cores. Younger typologies like grid cities have less use for such designs; sprawl cities almost none at all.

Boston is by colonial standards an old city and it has Route 128, initially a series of already existing streets that formed an inexact circuit around Boston and later a limited-access circumferential highway, the first of its kind in the nation, now, in the twenty-first century, a curving high-tech run, a silicon rally optimistically dubbed "America's Technology Highway"—but in 1972 it was a scungy corridor of doughnut shops and furniture stores, déclassé towns like Dedham and Lynnfield, nicer burbs like Newton and Milton. In the middle of the seventeenth century, the Long Parliament as part of its twenty-year deliberations formed "A Corporation for the Promoting and Propagating the Gospel of Jesus Christ in New England," a large part of whose funds found their way to the Puritan missionary John Eliot in the Massachusetts Bay Colony toward a grand Christianizing project. Eliot translated the Bible into the Massachusett language and founded a series of townships into which the natives were meant to move, having forsworn hunting and gathering for the gospel. In the end there were fourteen "praying towns," though only two had fully independent congregations: Ponkapoag and Natick, which would later be linked by the incomplete loop described by Route 128. The former is now the town called Canton at the highway's southern terminus, and the latter the town where in 1951, the very year that 128 was opened as a highway to immediate traffic jams, Jonathan Richman was born.

What bacterial warfare, religious fervor, and direct violence began, political economy completed. Waltham, just inside the ring road, is the original home of the Boston Manufacturing Company and its perfected power loom. It was there that Francis Cabot Lowell's textile mill unified under a single roof the chain of tasks that would convert raw cotton into finished cloth, pioneering mass production in no small part through the dramatic induction of women into the workforce, the Lowell Mill Girls, each working about eighty hours a week, the whole integrated shitshow to be known as the Waltham-Lowell System, the basis of American manufacture and all that flowed from it. The "system" thus brought together, with great expansionary gusto, the cheapest wage labor in the North with the slave labor of the South, to much celebration. It was one of the first great inventions of industrial capitalism; you can tell because they swiftly founded a newer and bigger factory town that they managed to name Lowell, which would be known as "the cradle of the American Industrial Revolution," a revolution that would transform all before it, would rise and fall, turning and turning and exhausting itself somewhere in and around 1972.

The year 1972 matters, and surely you will have seen this coming, because it is almost 1973, the year of massive industrial collapse, of the Watergate hearings and the United States' formal withdrawal from the humiliation in Southeast Asia, the final dissolution of the Bretton Woods monetary system setting the stage for increasing trade and current account imbalances—and this is just the start of the list, if you were driving the ring road named 1973, these are the things you would pass in the first few miles. It is almost 1973 but not quite when the song is written by a Boston teenager who performs it on the Cambridge Common playing a Jazzmaster adorned with stickers from Howard Johnson's hospitality chain and soon thereafter wanders into a record company bidding war that Warner Bros. wins, which is to say loses, after which he and some friends record "Roadrunner" and a few other songs for Cale, the Welsh bass player and keyboardist formerly of the Velvet Underground (VU). By the time these demos are released as an album by a different label altogether it will be two years after the band's farewell concert. It is already too late.

The friends who cut the demo do not include John Felice, original member and Jonathan's childhood friend who by 1972 had already left the band and would later recall how "We used to get in the car and we would just drive up and down Route 128 and the turnpike. We'd come up over a hill and he'd see the radio towers, the beacons flashing, and he would get almost teary-eyed."[1] It was said of Fra Angelico, the Italian painter of the early Renaissance, that "he never painted a Crucifix without bathing his own cheeks with tears; and therefore it is that the expressions and attitudes of his figures clearly demonstrate the sincerity of his great soul for the Christian Religion."[2] It's like that except for the Christianity part and the fact that Jonathan Richman never had a patron like Cosimo de' Medici. Felice cannot abandon this vision, he is captured by it, it drives around and around inside him and he repeats it as if he is saying something new and by the way that is the whole secret of popular culture right there, repeating something as if you are saying something new: "We'd drive past an electric plant, a big power plant, with all kinds of electric wire and generators, and he'd get all choked up, he'd almost start crying."[3]

That repetition, that improvisation on a theme, is also the shape of the song. The theme is, *What I saw while driving around.* But before this, the song opens with Richman's eccentric but plain count-in, "one two three four five six." The count is both obvious and strange, which is Greil Marcus's assessment of the whole thing, "the most obvious song in the world, and the strangest."[4]

The intuition, however, is always that we will not find an explanation for this verdict inside the song, that *obvious* and *strange* are lodged in relationships to the world and you start with the song to get to the world, you rise from the abstract to the concrete, which means you start with the six count and then the song introduces its title character, "Roadrunner Roadrunner," the narrator naming himself but not yet in the first person. It is not the cartoon creature who had been Wile E. Coyote's antagonist since 1949, not the character who takes the lead in Bo Diddley's twelve-bar blues circa 1960, but with the same name nonetheless and something like the same degree of simplification that attaches to those two, little phrase followed by three sharp strums of two fine chords which are the song's *beep beep*—"Roadrunner Roadrunner," D/D/A, and then comes the depthless figure of speech that sets the song apart from anything in its cohort, "going faster miles an hour," and it is tempting to get hung up on that invention, it has already happened and we are not yet ten seconds in, tempting for us but not for the song which does not hesitate but drives forward, D/D/A, "gonna drive past the Stop & Shop," D/D/A, "with the radio on."

It's a compact opening, eighteen words parceled out by syllable, 6, 8, 8, 6, because although the song is interested in rhyme only intermittently, it is very careful about *what happens when*—about how far we get in how much time, which just happens to be what velocity is. And the song's velocity is faster miles an hour. Faster than what? Faster than you were going before, faster than all the other rock songs, faster than sitting in your room. But none of those work, not really. It is a comparison without a comparator and it is meant to be, is meant to turn a specific relation of distance and time into a general experience. "Going fast," writes Kristin Ross about the advent of car culture and particularly the other side of the tedious commute that congeals time into an aspic, "has the effect of propelling the driver off the calendar, out of one's own personal and affective history, and out of time itself." It's transcendent, that is to say, a description of pop music's sublime discovered where the radio meets the road. Then she quotes the theorist Jean Baudrillard, who is not always wrong, "Mobility without effort constitutes a kind of unreal happiness, a suspension of existence," and then Jean makes a curiously specific claim, note the exact number as it will come back around: "At more than a hundred miles an hour, there's a presumption of eternity."[5] The song tracks this experience, not just the hypnosis of the highway but more broadly that great magic trick through which quantity is transmuted into quality, as if we could inhabit the perpetual relative, the inaccessible wanting, more, better, faster, except that *more* and *better* are both sort of avaricious and mean-spirited while *faster* is just . . . faster, that abstract wash of desire that we would like to feel concretely in the form of wind on a summer night, the blur of lights.

The blur of lights! If you do not get caught up in the metaphysics of faster miles an hour, then there is the Stop & Shop to capture your attention, that venerable Boston institution, well,

Somerville really, just as Howard Johnson's is from Quincy down the South Shore. The company takes the official name "Stop & Shop Inc." in 1942, the very same year that *Billboard* magazine first uses the term albeit with slightly archaic orthography. "rock-and-roll," just look at the names, Stop & Shop, rock & roll, one of them the other stood on its head. It is alluring to go down that road, to wonder which outpost Jonathan means, exactly, which Stop & Shop a teenager on the beltway could drive past around 1970. It could be a few different ones but a good guess would be the store on Elm Street in Woburn, just a few yards north of the Yankee Division Highway, as Route 128 of the Many Names is also called, whose sign would have been easily visible at any velocity. The one in Reading is also a real possibility. The firm's own corporate history sings of demographics and social transformations. The entry for the 1950s reads in its entirety, "We move out to the suburbs as the baby boom begins and new highways are built." They mean 128. Except shortly after the opening of "Once" but not of "Twice," after their nearly identical first verses, Jonathan for verse 2 of "Once" will sing or say—and these are the *same thing* says the song which is in so many ways about not being able to sing and also singing—he will sing or say, "I walked by the Stop & Shop, then I drove by the Stop & Shop." He hits "drove" a little. If you read that corporate website some more, it offers up just a bit greater detail: "In 1959, Stop & Shop opens its 100th store in Natick, MA."[6]

So then: hometown, good place to start a song, obvious really, and continuing the theme of comparison, he makes the clearest point available about driving, makes the rock & roll point, "I liked that much better than walking by the Stop & Shop," which almost doesn't need saying, given that we already know, given that this leap into the driver's seat makes the song possible, the leap into the modern world. But these unassailable facts still miss the crucial distinction between walking and driving in and around 1972, the basis for his preference, and he hurries the line a little to make it fit so he can arrive at its conclusion in a timely manner, "cuz I had the radio on."

This phrase is never a conclusion, though, it is part of the song's recursion and repetition, the radio song about radio songs, and he is in touch with the modern world, he is in love with the modern world, and then the second verse of "Once" returns to the territory, "I felt in love with Mattapan and Roslindale cuz I had the radio on." This will be more or less consistent throughout "Once," a somewhat greater attention to immediate specifics, to town names, Felice's power lines and electrical plant, "50,000 watts of power." In 1976, Nick Lowe, garage rock archivist, will begin the song "So It Goes" with the line "I remember the night the kid cut off his right arm in a bid to save a bit of power," who knows what that's about, continuing, "he got 50,000 watts . . . in a big acoustic tower." This may be the first scavenging from "Roadrunner"; it will not be the last.

The second verse of "Twice," conversely, is in love with modern moonlight, with Massachusetts more broadly, in love with the radio on. "Twice" finds its level here for the most part, not quite as filled with specific objects or places but never drifting off to generalities which would be the greatest betrayal the song could contemplate. Unlike "Once," and this is a great distinction between the versions, in the second verse of "Twice," he turns from his love for everything great and small on his strip of road to something more difficult if still familiar, "It helps me from being alone late at night." He says it again, "It helps me from being lonely late at night." This loneliness arrives late to "Once," practically an afterthought. Here it is a basic building block, a topic, and he promises, "I don't feel so bad now in the car, don't feel so alone," and in case you have forgotten why this is the case over the last three and a half lines, he's got the radio on like the road-runner that's right.

The dynamic here is perhaps more complicated than we have been led to believe by the song's simplicity. There are two categories that between them contain all that you can be in love with in the modern world. One of these is the things of suburban Massachusetts, bearers of the "personal and affective history" Ross suspects is lost to sheer speed, the towns and roads and grocery stores and signs, neon more broadly, these things that he drives past, or in the case of the highway, the conveyance past all these things. And the other is the radio, the sheer fact of it, "the power of the AM," and also the songs it plays, "modern rock & roll." Romantic love does not figure.

There is another early song credited to the Modern Lovers,

"Ride On Down The Highway," that is at once so similar and so crude even in comparison that you would guess it was something like a rough draft or abandoned demo of "Roadrunner," though it seems that they developed alongside each other as the sixties gave way to the seventies, just two songs about driving. These were the earliest songs, along with "Howard Johnson's" and "I Grew Up in the Suburbs."[7] "Ride Down On The Highway" used to close the live sets before the "Roadrunner" encore, its lyrics changing across gigs and its title drifting a little as well. Certain phrases endure. "Ride down on the highway," it advises repeatedly, "ride down past the fried chicken stand," and then "late at night ride on Route 128" and "ride down past neon signs." Massachusetts moonlight is mentioned. Same song, except for a couple of things. In the middle of the song, for reasons enigmatic, the jangle stills for a momentary and imaginative leap: "there's a stone wall in western Europe and I cry in the afternoon sometimes." It is hard to suppose he means something other than the Berlin Wall but equally hard to suppose he is overcome by the historical melancholy of the continent's partitioning. The wall though, no avoiding it, is the opposite of a ring road, its true enemy. Perhaps this is why Jonathan weeps. Just as suddenly, as if realizing he has lost his way, he returns to America and Americana: "but then I get refreshed by a Coca-Cola stand."

The other difference, this one far more significant than all the world-warring of the twentieth century, is that this singer in distinction to the one in "Roadrunner" has a girlfriend, one who while remaining abstract appears over and over, "my girl-friend has to promise on the highway by my side, girlfriend has to promise never to leave my side ever again." It's a lousy idea of what a girlfriend is, inherited from the radio.

Or maybe it is inherited from "car culture," that collection of images that gathered as much social force as any other in the era we are navigating, images striking not the least for their white-ness (though as we shall see it is the black motorist who stands at the origin of rock & roll, or sits behind the wheel), even more so for their offering up the automotive world as a sort of boy's town where women had only the most straitened options, two roles, not much distance between them. "Where women have not been used to eroticize cars as objects of desire," writes Grace Lees-Maffei, "they have been cast by the producers of car culture as figures of influence on purchases by men."[8] That this reduction to two roles in the world of images has not been particularly true in actuality has only the most limited bearing on how these things get figured. Moreover, if we make a break for it toward a purportedly egalitarian view that "the real emotional pull of the car is not sex, or social status, or all those things that we associate with car lovers," but is instead "that the motor car gives you the sense that you are a free person," that freedom has meant resoundingly different things for men and for women.[9]

There is no getting around the extent that Jonathan of Natick comes of age within this culture, this sense that the refuge of the roads is the preserve of the white male. "Ride On Down The

Highway" is marked and throttled by the limits of the automotive imagination. The song is interesting mostly because "Roadrunner" exists. "Roadrunner" exists to render "Ride On Down The Highway" superfluous, exists without that tedious form of romance, without that scaffolding or carapace, it mentions "modern girls" one time in "Twice" and no times in "Once" which by the standards of teenaged rock & roll, the standards that the song ceaselessly invokes and flouts, is no mention at all, less than zero. Françoise Sagan, another teen sensation as a novelist in midcentury France, saw early on the ménage à trois of boy and girl and car radio. "In Roger's car, she absent-mindedly switched on the radio," she writes of Paule, the lead character of *Aimez-vous Brahms . . .* , who then wonders out loud, "How many times have I done this before—turned on your car radio as you've driven me off to dinner?"[10] It is this trio that Jonathan reduces down to a pair, a boy and his radio, perhaps signaling a sort of sexual innocence that the found formula of "Highway" could not disguise, in any regard the most profound gesture of minimalism in a song where minimalism is the great principle, and for all that, still somehow expansive. Dion's great question "Why must I be a teenager in love?" is whirled around in the centrifuge of Route 128 and returns changed, charged with moonlight: *Why must I be a teenager in love with the modern world?*

So these are the two genres of love that this modern world comprises: common objects more and less commercial, and the radio. They have a peculiar relation, which is that the former things, despite Jonathan's great love for them, despite the evident delight they hold for him, leave him lonely and who knows why? Not despite their modernity but because of it. And here Jonathan Richman differs from Walter Benjamin: each thing he espies, no matter how mass-produced, no matter how embedded in the second nature that is the modern world, retains its authentic originality, its aura, the "unique phenomenon of a distance, however close it may be."[11] Hence his loneliness. In their very nearness they are distant. You come motorvating over the hill faster miles an hour and there is the world laid out before you in all its particulars, *right there* but unpossessable, and this is amplified by the fact that unlike the great feelings and the big ideas—we know those things are unpossessable, there is a lot of philosophy about that—the thing about real objects more and less commercial is that they sing of possession, of ownership, and that is part of their loneliness too. *Buy me, have me, take me home*, they would say if they could, but you can't, and you don't.

This is where the radio comes in, the radio in the car that rock & roll insists must always be nearby. It is a sort of balm on that loneliness; it does not repair it exactly but makes it okay. It fills in the space between Jonathan and the mute things of the world. This is the promise of the radio, of the pop song, it fills all space. You know the feeling, the one that comes over you upon hearing a song not for the first but the second time, after you have heard it once and the itch has begun, after you have started to suspect that you must hear that goddamned song again or expire, and then there it is, the thing that possesses you more intensely than anything else but that you can never possess, that evaporates before sunrise. We are at the end of the second verse. In both "Once" and "Twice," in the version that tilts toward cataloging the local and in the version that tilts toward loneliness and its salve, we are seventy seconds in.

We are in some sense trapped in the problem of the two versions, the problem of comparison. The second verses are different and have a different feeling. Another significant difference is that, after the third verse, which is more or less the same in both versions, there is an instrumental break in "Twice" that does not happen in "Once." and this break features an organ solo by Jerry Harrison, maybe twenty seconds exactly as crude as you would hope for, and also perfect in how it summons the nighttime solitude that inflects this version. Despite that, "Twice" is more than half a minute shorter than "Once." This is true in part because "Twice" is a few beats per minute faster, about 8 percent, which accounts for some but not all the difference in length. It feels fast. Well, "Once" feels fast too, but "Twice" feels faster.

It is easy, especially if you listen to them back-to-back as they appear on that 1977 seven-inch, to be struck by how different "Once" and "Twice" are, a sensation amplified by the oddity of having two different versions of a pop song in the first place both equally canonical, which also means both equally noncanonical, when you have grown accustomed to the perfectibility of the pop song. The whole point of pop is, they fuck around with it until they get it right, the band, the engineer and the producer, the label, and that's the single, that is the technology of the pop song as it develops across the century and especially after the introduction of the 45 rpm two years before Route 128 opens for business. You get the version that they got right, and a B-side. Even if that's a different take of the same song, it is subordinate to the original.

Sort of. The arguments against the possibility of isolating out an original in some authoritative way are many and hard to refute. There are remixes and radio edits and twelve-inch versions and covers, and while these multiples generally exist in a hierarchy, that hierarchy is not always simple. Any of these unoriginals might be remembered alongside or become better known than the original, can even be misremembered *as* the original, and this is ignoring the metaphysical question of what makes an original in the first place—is it the first recording, the first performance, the first time it is written down? There are all kinds of reasons that it is perverse to lean on the idea of the original in pop music.

Still, we are talking about a single. Not just a lone track as opposed to an album but *singular*, singular in its multiplicity, which is to say, when a million copies circulate, there is no unique original but there is a shared experience of hearing a single, you have the radio on and I have the radio on, we have more or less a single thing in common, the same way that if you and I look at the Stop & Shop sign in Woburn on a summer evening in and around 1972, we have that sign in common. There is something about a single. It exists in history. We might find confounding exceptions but exceptions are only arguments in logic class. If, meeting under that Stop & Shop sign on that summer evening, we happen to discuss "The First Time Ever I Saw Your Face," even though it was written in 1957, even though it was recorded several times thereafter, even though the Roberta Flack version first gained purchase though its appearance in a 1971 film about a disc jockey if you must know, even though the single that would be released in the spring of 1972 and later be awarded Grammy Record of the Year had been recorded in 1968, something something thing Nixon, even despite all this, we would be talking about the same song, same version.

This irresolvable argument goes a long way toward explaining why we lean instead on the idea of a canonical version, a matter of tacit agreement about which version is our starting point, even as we admit there may be many others, better, worse, different. A single isn't a heaven-given fact, it's a social relation. But even this can't resolve the puzzle of "Roadrunner." Perhaps this is because, despite what it seemed to promise to fans and label execs early on, and perhaps because of the fate of the Modern Lovers, and perhaps because of the fact that Jonathan Richman decided before any version was released that he wished to leave this sound behind entirely, a refusal in retrospect so extraordinary it is hard not to the think of the great artistic refusals of the nineteenth century—perhaps owing to all this the single never sold much at all, never charted in the United States, never had the chance to sew space and time together into the shared experience of everybody in the dark listening to the same thing. No one version became canonical. It is a single and not.

This is a part of the mystery of "Roadrunner." There is always not enough canon or too much. People are always getting the versions confused. Inevitably, one feels always compelled to *distinguish* between the versions, to be overly attentive to the specific differences I have begun to list, to difference overall. For all that, the two versions of "Roadrunner" are the same song. Really, *what I saw while driving around* and *why must I be a teenager in love with the modern world* pretty much cover it. But this combination is intimately new and it is the combination that makes the song, that opens up a space as wide as the night in and around 1972, a space made for the improvisations, which of course change version by version, night by night, without changing the song because that improvisation on that framework is what the song is. The remainder of the variation in length between the two versions comes from the fact that the last part of the song can be any length at all, unlike a verse structure or a melody, there is nothing regulating its length, nothing at all, and it is extended further in "Once," the band chanting "RADIO ON" while Jonathan pursues the theme of what he sees, what he loves, and what he's got, a device that will run out the track, entirely unfamiliar and yet entirely conventional, made from the most recognizable building blocks. Baudelaire wanted to say a cliché for the first time and it's like that, surely this is a convention you simply haven't heard yet, it feels like songs have been doing this forever, that this is what songs *are*, right?

And so begins the protean list, a last enumeration in a song of enumeration, he's got the AM, he feels alone in the cold and lonely, he's got the rockin' modern neon sound, modern neon modern sound, finally he mentions Boston, one time only, Boston town and Boston sound respectively. Toward the very end of "Twice" he says, "Late at night hit 'em wide with rock & roll late at night I've got—" and the Modern Lovers sing "RADIO ON" and Jonathan says "The factories and the auto signs" and he mumbles for a second and says "ALLLLLRIGHT" and that's it, a few seconds later, he pulls up on the guitar, bangs out a couple last chords, declares "Right, bye-bye" as simple as can be and we are out.

Variable in length, the song's ending passage is in all cases long enough, sometimes as long as the rest of the song, that it would be a mistake to call it an outro, a breakdown, a fade. It is just a part of the song, arguably the main part, inarguably the part that will most seep into pop music and rise to the surface here and there, more and less obviously, forever. But I am getting ahead of myself.

We have skipped over the third verse and it is here that the song breaks open. It happens just like this. "Said hello to the spirit of 1956" it begins, "patient in the bushes next to '57." In a song of plain speech this is, like "faster miles an hour," a fanciful figuration. We are driving through time or past time. "The highway is your girlfriend as you go by so quick" (aha! it turns out there is a girlfriend in the song after all), then "Suburban trees, suburban speed and it smells like heaven." There's a rhyme for you, seven and heaven, the most clichéd rhyme on offer this side of fire and desire and this is the point, things have been purified down to the crude minimum of rock & roll, the guitars back off, even the drums for a second, all those moves that signal this is the bravura moment where the singer shouts something. But there is no shouting. Instead, Jonathan says, "Roadrunner once, roadrunner twice, I'm in love with the modern world and I'll be out all night." That's in "Twice." "Once" has it plural: "We're in love with this feeling now and we'll be out all night." It is somewhere between ecstatic and laconic. The song slides from verse form into the "RADIO ON" form like the slide from the lights of Natick into the dark of the turnpike. It is as close to a chorus as the song will get.

Earlier I offered up a foundational story for rock & roll, a folktale. Let us revisit it, not for the last time. There is a music lover but not a professional musician. They are adjacent to the radio. One day they encounter an ordinary object, a popular object, but they see its beauty, they encounter it with a sort of religious fervor, and they see that the world is filled with these things, that the world is thus itself beautiful. It is a sort of revelation. And they have a need to deliver this message about their love for the world, about the extraordinariness of the ordinary, and they see that a pop song is the way to do this because a pop song is, like a highway, both a perfect conveyance and a perfect example of this sort of ordinary, popular, beautiful thing. So they put this all into a song, a song that is their message to you that they are prepared to drive around the world or at least around the ring road to deliver, and though they are not much of a singer they begin to sing. Now I will make the obvious additions. "Roadrunner" is the incomparable and illimitable version of this story. It has never been told this purely, this relentlessly, lifting out of itself to communicate this one thing. In this regard, lacking a verse-chorus structure, lacking a chord progression, lacking a melody, lacking, it would seem, a working knowledge of what a song is, it is for all that the most conventional song ever recorded.

And yet "Roadrunner" is not the story of rock & roll in some mythic sense and it is not some reduction to an abstract and general situation meant to be universally applicable and familiar. Or it is, but it achieves its spectral universality through its insistence on particulars. Not just proper names. It is a story about a particular time and a place, about the American era that rock & roll signifies. It is set within that and cannot be disentangled. It is almost 1973, the year of the oil crisis and gas rationing, the end of the greatest economic expansion known to humans, and I mention this because everything that begins also ends, childhood, the Holy Roman Empire, the Hundred Years' War, feudalism, the period during which Joni Mitchell was transcendent, *Gravity's Rainbow*, rock & roll, and capitalism too, this is an absolute certainty, capitalism will end as everything in history ends. And within that great arc, the American Industrial Revolution has already in and around 1972 come to a close and "Roadrunner" is among other things the song of that ending.

It is almost 1973 but not quite and Jonathan Richman is driving the ring road, faster miles an hour, and the price of gas is the farthest thing from his mind, he has the radio on and he's going around and around, the guitar is going around and around, the lyrics are going nowhere for the simple reason that there is no particular place to go, just around and around, and he passes the spirit of 1956, the commanding heights of the postwar boom, and the homely suburbs are in full bloom, and although it's *close* to the birth of rock & roll, it's the *exact* year of the largest public works project in American history, which is of course the Federal-Aid Highway Act, all $25 billion of it, the birth of the Interstate Highway System, *fucking infrastructure* just like the Stop & Shop and the Howard Johnson's and the radio towers are fading remnants from the world of *stuff*, and this is why it's the greatest song of the era, because rock & roll is the last great invention of industrial capitalism and "Roadrunner" is a love song for the world of industrial capitalism when it's late at night, and then Jonathan passes the spirit of 1957, he turns around in the night and is consumed by neon.

▶ 03 That Highway Sound, 1955

"ROADRUNNER" IS INEXHAUSTIBLE, maybe that is what I have been trying to say. It tells that one story, the ur-story, over and over, same two chords, same simple song, Jonathan is always never playing it again, he is always playing it again. Indeed, to this point we have not discussed the existence of a third version, less canonical but enough to get its own determiner, a live recording made sometime after he first renounced the song, the version known as "Roadrunner (Thrice)" that appeared as a B-side in 1977.

In "Hospital," another early song, he sings, "I go to bakeries all day long, there's a lack of sweetness in my life." You can hear this as a guiding principle in "Thrice," a principle that has won the day against older versions. You can hear his renunciation of the spirit of 1972, his renunciation of "Roadrunner" even as he is playing "Roadrunner." He is neither the first nor the last artist to conclude that a style is an ethics, and while one may disagree with the outcome, one cannot fault the commitment. "And I'm in *love*," he says sweetly in "Thrice," passing towns and places in the night, "with the land where I grew up." Really holding the vowel into a croon, that comic but extremely not ironic croon that will provide one of the coordinates for his later career, he says again, "And I'm in *loooove*," and then with great tenderness he retracts something once basic to the song. "Well you might say I feel lonely," as if it had been our idea all along and not something he had intimated line by line since the song's origins, "but I wouldn't say I feel lonely, I would say that I feel alive all alone." *In love*, *alive*, *alone*, he is really going to town on these sounds, trying to remake a meaning from the slightest variations.

But he has taken back the lonely only halfway, reinterpreted it. He always said, after all, that the radio helped him from being lonely. It's the same feeling, that *alone in the car with the radio on* feeling, he just understands it differently now, this great circumnavigation in the dark. He doesn't mind that he's alone, he sings himself into a sort of trance. "Thrice" is almost as long as "Once" and "Twice" laid end to end and the circuit it rides reaches correspondingly further, in sight of downtown Boston, down to the South Shore, looping around. For all its expansion it is all the more reduced, for long stretches little more than gentle electric guitar, some percussion barely audible behind it. "I'm hypnotized" he says three times, and he rolls clear out to western Massachusetts along the Turnpike through fields of snow. "Now the first of December was covered with snow, so was the turnpike from Stockbridge to Boston," James Taylor had sung in 1970, heading west to east, and Jonathan reverses the course followed by "Sweet Baby James" but the genre is right, "Thrice" is a lullaby, the genre of sweetness itself, a reverse lullaby to keep himself awake. He drives for a couple of hours until "the college out there just rises in the middle of nothing," almost certainly the University of Massachusetts, Amherst, and its University Tower Library, begun in 1972 naturally and completed two years later, the tallest academic research library in the world.

There is something satisfying for a listener, unknowable and complicit passenger, in figuring these things out—something satisfying in deciding that one thing the song is for, in its various guises, is to reconstruct an era and a landscape, a world, the contours of existence for a teenager in suburban Massachusetts in the seventies. The British journalist Laura Barton traveled to the United States in 2007 and endeavored to re-create the route, or all the routes, to identify the landmarks still standing from "a minor UK hit 30 years ago this week."[1] This seems like a plausible thing to do; the song across all its versions is an archival resource in that way. The library that rises before Jonathan will later be renamed for W. E. B. Du Bois, his archives stored there. Du Bois was from Great Barrington, just eight miles down the highway from the Stockbridge of "Sweet Baby James," if you really bombed it you might get from one town to the other in the time it takes to listen to "Thrice" and though Jonathan can know none of this in 1977, it is hard not to stop short at all that this knowledge conjures. "Roadrunner" is not a song that has a lot to say about its own whiteness, though another way to say the same thing is that it speaks it incessantly. The song's ambit is not just "suburban" but the surround that this entails, the suburban world midway along the arc of white flight, in the shadow of post–civil rights desegregation initiatives and violent reactions thereto, national events that found their most toxic expression right there in Boston: the so-called busing crisis, in reality white riots against school integration that lasted from 1974 to 1976, the years that separate the recordings of "Once" and "Twice" from their release. The seventies suburbs lining Route 128 mean this if they mean anything at all.

But the song does not pause in Boston as it does not pause at the library. It is not a song that pauses, it comes back around, a 45, a ring road, repetitive, infinite. "Repetition without tedium is the backbone of rock and roll," writes Robert Christgau, in and around 1972, not about Jonathan Richman but about Chuck Berry.[2]

Chuck Berry doesn't appear in "Roadrunner." No singers appear, and no songs, not by name. In a song whose content concerns what it is to be in love with rock & roll, to have the radio on, and whose form is extreme enumeration of particulars, a song that comes slathered with proper names, this is an omission so obvious as to be almost invisible. Once you notice the absence, the missing library at the heart of the song, it becomes part of what the song is about. We can only speculate, and given that the song is a fiction, such speculations are double fictions. We are already in the *terra infirma* of art; we should beware of wandering into the neighboring realm of the counterfactual. What if he also passes a Star Market? He doesn't, he passes a Stop & Shop; the song says so and it doesn't say otherwise. A song's actuality is what is given, why pretend otherwise?

But that is what it is to think with a song. *Something* is playing on the radio, several somethings over the course of a night driving around, and we have some hints. We have some hints in how the song sounds and how it feels and how it's shaped. We know that the key word "rocking" means not just side to side but around and around because Chuck Berry said so in 1958: "They say the joint was rocking, going 'round and 'round." It is a blues B-side that would enter the rock canon not least because that is what the Rolling Stones played during their 1964 debut on the *Ed Sullivan Show* as part of the transnational project to simultaneously remember and forget where rock & roll had come from. "Around and Around" is a club song about going to a club, with a quick, clean guitar figure to open, the kind of invention that Berry tossed off every week in and around 1958. Everybody is having a good time, reeling and rocking to that crazy sound, until the cops show up. Even that doesn't stop them; they never stop rocking until the moon goes down, because that is what it means to go around and around.

While the Stones busied themselves with admiring covers, Berry released "No Particular Place to Go," a single that opens with another quick guitar riff, this one more like a chime. Dated 1964, the song is possessed by the spirit of 1957 quite literally, its music recycled from that year's "School Days." In the original, Berry gives the opening chime its narrative sense by singing "ring! ring! goes the bell," a phrase that eventually arrives at its opposite pole, "hail! hail! rock & roll," but the 1964 version goes in a different direction, answering the chime with all the exposition that Berry will ever need: "Riding along in my automobile, my baby beside me at the wheel."

It is a song about driving around while trying to make it with his paramour over there in the passenger seat, unsafely busying himself trying to unfasten her, uh, seatbelt while in motion, an episode—"the safety belt that wouldn't budge"—that becomes the song's comic centerpiece. Comedy begets invention. As he frustrates himself with her clasp, he growls, "*Riiiiding* along in my calaboose, still trying to get her belt a-loose," and it is perhaps not until the second or third time that you realize that *calaboose* isn't a word for *car* that you recognize even if it is clear from context, from its echo of the opening line, from its similarity to *caboose* and *cabriolet*. It turns out to be an Americanization of the Spanish word for a dungeon, *calabozo*, endeavoring to amplify the comedy via the proposition that the cabin of your vehicle, freedom itself, is a jail cell if you cannot undo the locks of sex.

That is one story. There is another one, the story in which Berry writes the song while in jail, eighteen months in '62 and '63 for violating the Mann Act, a sentence that is on the one hand notable for its racist character and on the other hand one fiber in the skein that is Berry's mistreatment of women. Skein may undersell things, maybe a lea or a spyndle. Art is fiction but it is a grim thought that Berry's high-speed teen idylls performed a very specific act of dissembling, a raucous veil over decades of well-documented predation. Something happens within that sustained sleight of hand, something ugly and true. Ann Powers has written perceptively of the extent to which Berry depended on the ideal image of the real teenaged girls who made rock & roll happen, not dragooned muses so much as tastemakers, audiences, listeners in the dark of the concert hall, "the women who stood at its door, took the tickets, wrote the informal accounts in their fan letters, told the DJs what to play."[3] That truth is always with rock, compressed, disguised, and displaced, idealized forever as "my baby beside me," the woman in the passenger seat—and when I wrote last chapter that "Roadrunner" as a song exists "without that tedious form of romance," there is a sense in which that can never be true. Richman's song tests out what it would mean to live without it. It says, tenderly, if there must be a girlfriend, let it be the highway. This is his distance from Berry. Meanwhile Berry's history—the conditions in which "No Particular Place to Go" is written, his second single out of prison and his highest-charting song of the decade—diminishes its humor but not its formal concision found at every turn, never more than when he rounds on the first refrain, "cruisin' and playin' the radio, with no particular place to go."

So these are two pieces of "Roadrunner," if we are now snapping it together from parts, from songs we can imagine Jonathan hearing in our counterfactual game, "Around and Around," and

"No Particular Place to Go." And that turns out to be all that *he* will need. People will later say that "Roadrunner" is minimalist because it has only two chords and a droning feel, will associate this with a sort of art-rock reduction. They will note the song's similarity to "Sister Ray." There is no doubt that Richman loved the Velvet Underground, studied their sound, sought out Lou Reed, hung out with the group. Even that relationship was vehicular: "Occasionally, I drove them around in my father's car," he said (the father in question a traveling salesman; the Richmans have gasoline for blood).[4] He would later name a song after the band. Said genealogy is a reasonable thing to believe, especially if you buy the standard line about the broad and enduring influence of VU. The seeming formlessness of the lyrics to "Roadrunner," no verse no chorus, is matched by the music's resistance to formal completion, just an *A* and a *D* making up between them the song's great partiality, frustrating the conventional vocabulary of I-IV-V with that mostly missing *E*, the song's great absence— the sustained I-IV that remains providing a feeling that there is something out there that is not named, not seen, not known or knowable. It would be reasonable to call it avant-pop. A composer friend of mine writes about this chord structure, "It's almost as if there is a *thereness* to the *here*."[5] That captures something true about the song, the way that it is finally more interested in what is beyond the headlights, flickering in the night.

"He loved the Velvet Underground—he loved two bands—the Stooges and the Velvets," says Ernie Brooks, original bassist on "Twice," "and that's what's funny about Jonathan, his music didn't sound like either band, but there was some deep connection there." It is at this point in the interview that this "funny" ambivalence blossoms. "He also loved the Velvet Underground, but he was very conflicted about them, because of the darkness they presented. I always had this theory that our sound was almost the opposite of the Velvets, that basically we were playing into the light as opposed to the darkness."[6] This sense is prevalent. The journalist Lisa Robinson, tracing the influence of vu on the New York scene and in particular on Talking Heads, can't help but mention our modern lover. But not because he is the same, quite the reverse, as Robinson notices immediately: "The boy lead singer David Byrne is like Jonathan Richman without the warmth."[7]

Darkness and light, cold and warmth. This is perhaps the great secret, obvious as it is: Modern Lovers are the contradiction of vu, complementary, conjoined, but *opposite*. The Velvet Underground, one might say, are metarock, a knowing take on genre and its conventions, not insincere but relentlessly ironic in the sense of reflecting back on their own form, *rock & roll* forever in italics, immensely satisfying to the class for whom knowing better is always a primary virtue, and there is something insightful in how early they saw that the rock genre was already formalized, calcified even, that the Beatles and Stones hadn't started anything so much as finished it, realized its ambitions, and as Rabbi Hillel says, the rest is commentary. In this regard, vu shares a secret affinity with the band Boston, whose aforementioned radio-friendly seventeen-million-unit shifter is remarkable for the fact that each of its eight tracks is a good song, every single goddamned one of them, and despite this or because of this, the album is terrible, declaring over the course of thirty-eight minutes a dismal knowledge, a dismal fact, that rock & roll is solved, that there is no longer a mystery. It is pure metarock and they knew it. "We were just another band out of Boston," they sing in a song that you will not be surprised to hear is called "Rock & Roll Band," "on the road and trying to make ends meet."

"Roadrunner" is the opposite of metarock. It is an anti-irony campaign. It has no interest in knowing better, in solving the mystery, in knowing anything other than what it discovers along the highway. You might say there are two rock minimalisms: Velvet Underground minimalism and Chuck Berry minimalism. One is a formalism that cuts across all of the arts, sculptors and painters and conceptualists, the other a world picture that rock & roll develops, both of them mediated by sound but neither able to be exhausted by sound alone. The opposition is everywhere. Jerry Harrison said, reflecting on 1973 again: "Jonathan had switched to a new style of guitar that didn't use much distortion. . . . He'd still play, but kind of as he does now, little Chuck Berry riffs, generally a far cleaner sound. There's like the great divide in Jonathan's guitar playing between the time when he's trying to emulate Sterling Morrison and Lou Reed and when he decided that he did like Chuck Berry—up until then he hated Chuck Berry."[8]

But this gives too much to guitar tone, gives too much to the clean historical break, the kind with a before and an after. The story of "Roadrunner" eludes such narration with its multiple versions, its renunciations and returns, its circling around and around. It is more persuasive to hear the song as itself a transition— not a solution but a process, a way of figuring something out, and this is why there can be no singular version. *It is the single that is multiple.* If it sets its sights on the past, it is hard to hear a desire to go back, say, to 1965, to the moment that VU meets Warhol, signs with Verve. No, it is clear about this, it says so out loud, it wants to get back to the origin, the ur, not metarock that knows itself too well but protorock that has just now figured something out maybe for the first time, that begins as an absolute simplification of the given, getting everything it needs by assembling *car*, *highway*, *aimless circularity*, *loneliness*, *nighttime*, *rock & roll radio*, it says that this is the entire world, is everything you need, beauty, truth, truth, beauty, all that song and dance, and the way it becomes possible at this particular moment, not in and around 1972, not 1965, but in 1956, spirit of.

The year 1956 is patient in the bushes next to '57, when Chuck Berry writes a song beginning "They're really rocking in Boston," a phrase that was at one point planned as the first line of this book except that it opens what is arguably Berry's most unforgivable song in its handling of teen girls, the song being "Sweet Little Sixteen," whose music is not much later scrubbed clean in the California sun and returns as the Beach Boys' "Surfin' U.S.A."

Car song, surf song, not much distance between them: "We'll all be planning out a route, we're gonna take real soon."

If the two tracks, "Sixteen" and "Surfin'," have one or several distances between them, they both offer rock & roll as a way to imagine *nation*, a series of disparate spots joined in an emerging network. What unifies them? That is the question. Or as Berry's "Back in the U.S.A." poses the matter, "Did I miss the skyscrapers, did I miss the long freeway?" Or "New York to East California" as Kim Wilde will later summarize matters in a song with the least surprising title in history, "Kids in America."

It is in the catchment and penumbra of 1956 that this partic-ular alchemy we can call car culture or youth culture or rock & roll discovers its material conditions, the gradual and then extra-ordinary world making whose signature is the authorization of the Interstate Highway System, almost fifty thousand miles from coast to coast, from the Beach Boys Historic Monument hard on the 105 in Hawthorne, California, all the way to the Mass Pike running through Natick and on into Boston, and somewhere in between, Route 70 just north of Sumner High in St. Louis, where Chuck Berry played his first show, a highway system that we must admit is laid into the landscape for reasons other than the inven-tion of what we might call Cars on 45, reasons other than to make sure that first Berry and then the Wilson Brothers and then Jon-athan could drive around with the radio on.

There is a story that Dwight Eisenhower, having crossed the country via army convoy in 1919, and having encountered Germany's Reichsautobahn during World War II, saw the military virtue of such a system and that this is its reason for being. This is true in the way that it is true that Paris's wide boulevards were formed in the nineteenth century to ease the passage of troops, which is to say, not true, not really. Just as the Parisian boulevards were more accurately broadened to facilitate the passage of deliveries and of strolling consumers through what had recently been the crowded popular quarters now displaced by bourgeois commercial districts, the Interstate Highway System was the Great Circulator, designed to make sure that the products of the massively productive postwar factories could be brought to and from market with the ease and velocity they required, an ease and velocity that the streamlined and souped-up automobiles were happy to signify, the Cadillac Coupe de Villes and v8 Fords lending their charisma to impersonal megatons of asphalt and tar, having borrowed it just moments before from the Long Boom itself. Is not "repetition without tedium," Christgau's axiom for rock & roll, the pure logic of shopping? Repetition *with* tedium, now that's just another name for work, the assembly line and cotton field, domestic chores and the chain gang. But the Miracle Mile and the like? Passing this store and that, each with its own sign, its own promises, each one purring the same thing to passersby, *stop and shop*, some version of that—is this not the night around Jonathan, shopping itself in all of its presence and exhaustion, its signs now faded, its windows no longer gleaming, the world of commodities and their remnants grown somehow trivial and therefore beautiful? He takes the measure of this world from his car with something like love, the world of shopping whose real tedium waits always behind its promise, and if we know one thing for certain, know it from the shape and patter of the song, from the entirety of its vehicle, we know he is not going to stop.

He is not going to stop because, as surely as cars are a way of getting to the world, a consumption item and a way to consume, they are also a way of being in the world and a way that world is made. "In the middle of this century," offers Ross about the twentieth, "the automobile industry, more than any other, becomes exemplary and indicative; its presence or absence in a national economy tells us the level and power of that economy."[9] Not just a commodity but *the* commodity, the one by which others are measured, by which the modern world is measured. In the year before 1956, "car sales rose 37 percent in one year, vehicle production in the United States neared 10 million, unionized autoworkers won a forty-hour work week and health benefits, and the percentage of employees in unions peaked at over a third."[10] It is this world too, complement to the corridors of consumption, the world of production at its peak in 1955 and hollowing in 1972, that Jonathan marks out in the last moments of "Twice," the factories and the auto signs. The car is the Industrial Revolution achieved, the global order with America at its center, the car and the highway and the highway sound. The v8 Ford dates to 1932, the Cadillac Coupe de Ville debuts in 1949, FM radio leaps from the living room to the dashboard in 1952, national wealth has begun to tuck a few bills in the pockets of teenagers and now everything is in place, all the conditions, the constellation of objects and forces, and consequently, Christgau explains, "pop music is still understood to have changed utterly around 1955."[11] He means "Maybellene," more or less.

There is a debate about "Maybellene." Or, rather, there are various debates in which "Maybellene" features. The grandest one of them concerns whether it might be the first rock & roll song. "One of the first," says one encyclopedia, properly circumspect. There are competing claims: people will talk about "Rock Around the Clock" or "That's All Right" both from 1954, Jackie Brenston and his Delta Cats' 1951 song "Rocket 88," Big Mama Thornton's "Hound Dog" from the same year. Greil Marcus in *Lipstick Traces* floats the Orioles' 1948 song "It's Too Soon to Know," which is a brilliant choice if for no reason other than the entendre, *it's too soon to know what the first rock & roll song is*; it will always be too soon to know. Settle on any one of these and you are immediately fucked. "Rocket 88," which was in truth the first recording by Ike Turner's Kings of Rhythm, draws after all on "Cadillac Boogie" and "Rocket 88 Boogie," while "Maybellene" is a revision of the 1938 version of "Ida Red" by Bob Wills and his Texas Playboys, and there are other and older Ida Reds that give onto that one. Anyone who takes a position in these debates is bound for sorrow, a fact well known to all students of first things, as it is in the nature of origins to recede—once one is established, hammered into the rock face of tradition, it provides not just the desire but the position from which to discover another earlier origin, and then another, as all of us historians amateur and professional proceed piton by piton into the past.

But maybe it's "Maybellene."

There is something satisfying about the choice, and *satisfaction* may turn out to be a useful standard given that *truth* is not on offer. After decades of rock historiography in which white artists obscured the black artistry on which they drew in more or less shady fashion, and were given credit for inventing a genre when that credit economic and aesthetic belonged elsewhere, the story of Berry fashioning rock & roll out of Wills's 2/4 Western swing clicks into place charismatically. This story too, a vision of rock as black art, must be a simplification—but a useful one, a proportionate one, offering the classical virtue of symmetry, the dialectical pleasure of inversion, the ethical justice of redress.

This is not the only basis on which one might forward an argument for "Maybellene." There is genealogy and then there is history. By which I mean, to return to a theme, that one can only get so far in capturing how a song came into being, in grasping a song as a social fact, by tracking down its forerunners, its sources, its lineage—by understanding a song as a consequence of other songs. There are two evident limits to this approach that come to the fore in debates about the origins of genre. One is that the supposition that art comes from other art preserves an illusory autonomy of the cultural from the social, it seals off artistic making from how daily life is lived. The other is a version of what philosophers call the paradox of the heap, which offers a puzzle about sand, to wit, one grain of sand is not a heap, two grains are not a heap, three grains still nope, so at what point can we say we have a heap? If we follow the genealogical route, at what point of adding this rhythm and that attitude, this guitar sound and that way of singing, does a song become a new genre?

The historical method seeks to transcend both of these limits. Instead of peering backward along the sight line of culture, it presumes that songs and genres are also, emphasis on also, outcomes of the conditions in which they arise, not so much outcomes of specific events as of the great concatenation of forces and relations and experiences that make up our shared social existence. And so we could say that the necessary conditions for rock & roll are not the prior existence of "Ida Red" or "Cadillac Boogie" or the chance discovery of guitar distortion but are instead the very ones we have already named and of course many more, the constellation of life as it was lived in Memphis or Baltimore or St. Louis where Berry grew up, a city whose population peaked just a year or two before "Maybellene" and then began its long decline, first as a result of you guessed it highway construction and car ownership allowing mostly white outmigration into St. Louis County, and continuing as deindustrialization set in, that is what it means to say that rock & roll is the last great invention of industrial capitalism which exhausts itself on the road between 1955 St. Louis and 1972 Natick.

I am not really trying to make a case for the first rock & roll song because that is a rube's game. Certainly "Rocket 88" gets us into the car, a high-powered new production model, "ridin' all around town for joy." The joy part is important, drinking and cruising, the separation of the car from the unsayable fact of the factory that produced it, the separation of the joyrider from the brutalized assembly line worker even if they must in truth be the exact same person, consumer and producer, the separation between the two figures existing only as a preferred fiction for bourgeois economics and perhaps a necessary fiction for the life of the worker if pleasure is to be experienced as something other than the B-side of misery, even if that means accepting the devastating division of your capacities into work and leisure with the corollary that you can never be, you know, *a whole person*. This division is a necessity for rock & roll's existence, I am trying to say, and so is the dream that you can stand outside of it. In some sense this is what *teenager* means, not an age but a position. Sure school is a kind of factory, that is sort of Berry's point with "ring! ring! goes the bell," but this is what must in general be concealed for the romance of the teenager to blossom. You have a driver's license but no time card, not yet, and that is everything, physical speed but not the dreary commute. The teenager is the person not yet divided into two parts. The teenager accords with rock & roll's fantasy. There must be a car but it must be forever in the realm of consumption, going around and around. "It takes a fast car, lady," sang the Cars in 1979, "to lead a double life," but they are mistaken: all adults lead a double life, no car is fast enough either to draw the two together or to split them apart. It takes a fast car, maybe, to lead a single life. That's why teenagers are always riding around for joy.

The case for "Rocket 88" is not however complete. Perhaps it has something like the rock & roll sound, even if it is ruled by boogie-woogie piano and sax. It has the car, the joyride, but by midcentury there have been streets and towns and cars for some time, car songs dating back to the century's first hours. What changes for rock & roll is the arrival of the highway as a new order of things, as a system of nation and capital, not quite homogenizing so much as knitting the uneven landscape together, the highway as a version of the pop charts, the highway as the condition for the true continentalization of mass culture, as the stage where the action happens. I mean, Jonathan originally wrote out about twenty possible names for his band, Jonathan Richman's Rockin' Roadmasters, the Rock and Roll Dance Band, the Suburban Romantics, before settling on the full name of The Modern Lovers, the Danceband of the Highways, that's how it all started.[12]

Except it started years before. "Maybellene" sings of a contest between a woman and the singer that is just as much a race between two cars out on the highway, just as will Bo Diddley's "Roadrunner" a handful of years later with Diddley's roadrunning man proclaiming himself "the fastest in the land," no surprise there, and just as will "Fun, Fun, Fun" a few years after that with Carl Wilson's guitar homage to "Johnny B. Goode" and "Roll Over Beethoven" focusing on a female driver who "makes the

Indy 500 look like a Roman chariot race now."[13] Faster miles an hour. Speed matters.

Speed matters and speed kills, it's the flip side of fun fun fun. The highway song holds within it a fatal crash, that mournful microgenre of teen tragedy born just a few months after "Maybellene" with "Black Denim Trousers and Motorcycle Boots," a weeper going nowhere in the fall of 1955 when James Dean's fatal wreck sent it scaling the charts, Leiber and Stoller's first Top 10. From that point, entries come thick and fast, peaking early with songs like Mark Dinning's "Teen Angel" in 1959, written by his sister and her husband, the fifties were weird. The first verse begins, "That fateful night." It is always a fateful night in this precinct. Everyone gets in on the deadly action, even the Beach Boys with "A Young Man Is Gone," their effort outshone for once by their understudies Jan and Dean's "Dead Man's Curve," both tunes trivial compared to Wayne Cochran's "Last Kiss" or the epochal melodrama of the Shangri-La's "Leader of the Pack." It is a tradition that will eventually include no less than four songs called "Car Crash," none more memorable than the Avengers' 1977 version, same year as "Thrice," seeking to unmake twenty-two years of ultrapoignant excess with Penelope Houston's punk howl: "Dreamt you had a car crash, now you're dead on the road with your head smashed!" History is hard to howl away. Born with the Interstate Highway System, the car crash song is not just parallel but party to the rise of rock & roll, serving paradoxically as both the end and the guarantor of the freedom that the highway promises. If the teen provides an ideal of pure consumption freed from the drudgery of the worksite, the teen tragedy preserves this ideal forever in the amber of pathos and pure velocity, jammed with broken heroes never to return from the highway.

The microgenre also features, let it not go unsaid, the rescue, through the good graces of death, of youth from the anguishes and tawdriness of adult sexuality, and this it shares with "Roadrunner"—but not much else. On Route 128 it is in no regard a fateful night. And still it is absolutely exceptional, that is the song's conjuring trick, the music and the night extraordinary in their ordinariness. Nothing happens, and consequently we can be assured nothing will happen the next time that Jonathan is out on the ring road going around and around, that this night will last forever not through any magic but because it will be repeated again and again, Once, Twice, Thrice, such is its wish.

The crash hovers, perhaps, around "Maybellene," but it never happens. Berry's song has no interest in allegory or melodrama, its speed is in no way metaphorical. Moments suggest the story is a pursuit within the erotic convention, but mostly it seems like the goal of each party is not to couple up but to outrun the other, catching and then passing, the characters indexed so intensely to their vehicles that by the end it is easy to misrecognize "Maybellene" as the name of the Cadillac and not its driver.

It begins, after an opening chorus on loan from twelve-bar blues, with the gambit, "As I was motorvatin' over the hill." The pace is breakneck, the lyrical invention is impeccable, the race is on. The remainder tracks the duel of Cadillac Coupe de Ville and v8 Ford, hers new and upscale, his older and popular, a popular car just like popular quarters and popular song, signifying not just Ford but Fordism, the industrial order in its achieved form, the industrial worker who appears as something else entirely, just a driver, footboard-loose and fancy free. We are not quite sure where they are but outside town, "the open road," that is to say, very much where "Rocket 88" isn't. Chuck Berry is the poet of the Interstate Highway System, nothing less, the blacktop smoothed and straightened enough that you can crank it up over one hundred, which is exactly what happens, ninety-five miles per hour they're bumper to bumper, side to side, and then she starts to pull away as his engine overheats. It is here that nature intervenes and the rain comes down.

This is an irony passing by at high speed, the long record of songs in which rain arrives as divine rescue, a tradition that draws its power entirely from agrarian life and agricultural economies, from the threat posed to survival by natural conditions, by drought and with it crop ruination, starvation, impoverishment, bank foreclosure. This redemptive rain is a country music commonplace, the thing you pray for so you don't lose your land, preserved for example in the Steve Earle song called, naturally, "The Rain Came Down," where it falls in the chorus "like an angel coming down from above." That song sets its narration in the deep national past—homesteading, settling a piece of land (the settler aspect wholly uninspected), standing your ground—until in the final verse, after the turnaround, we leap into the song's present, the time after the rain could save you, after the changes that have rendered the family farm anachronistic, and our narrator finds himself at his doorway with the sheriff in the brutal closing couplet: "don't you come around here with your auctioneer man, 'cause you can have the machines but you ain't takin' my land." You can hear the shotgun by the door.

"Maybellene" is the century's turnaround. Our driver keeps the machine but not the land. There is no land in the way that the agrarian world understood it, it has been paved over and, more so, stripped of its meaning. The wagon train and the family farm have yielded to the highway and the factory, the farmer's market to the Stop & Shop. When the rain comes down on our driver's v8 Ford, the United States rests at its absolute peak of industrial employment while agriculture has descended from employing 80 percent of the U.S. work force to one in ten and falling fast, a great exodus from one labor sector to another which is also a geographical exodus particularly for black Americans, the Great Migrations that populated St. Louis, that populated Ford's St. Louis Assembly Plant cranking away in Hazelwood at the moment the song is written.

Is it too much to say that this is Berry's Du Bois moment, to say that the rock & roll synthesis requires this particular double-consciousness? Perhaps. Certainly it is the moment at which rock & roll must, to become itself, know as much about country & western as it does about rhythm & blues, in the way that American blackness must, to survive, know as much about whiteness as it does about itself. Chuck Berry, I mean to say, in order to do something very close to founding rock & roll, must know as much about 1955 America as anybody, know about the urban/rural divide which is a proxy for two entirely different economies with distinct relations to weather, work, land, machines, and if the rain can no longer rescue the farm, our driver is nonetheless rescued, "rainwater blowin' all under my hood, I know that was doin' my motor good," and then chorus solo chorus during which the almighty motor is resurrected, the turnaround that delivers us to the last verse.

At the end of the song, as you might expect, he catches Maybellene, returning us to the erotic story as we expect, but that is not what happens immediately after the break, when we learn instead that "the motor cooled down, the heat went down, and that's when I heard that highway sound."

And that is the other thing previously missing from the nascent genre, missing from "Rocket 88": not just the highway but the highway *sound*. It is an ambiguous phrase, as it must be to do the work of *making genre*. It cannot be (but it is!) both the first usage and a perfectly understood and complete meaning, a paradox of origins we have not seen the last of. A friend wonders if the highway sound is always a police siren, and it is hard to avoid that thought, but there is no other sign of the cops in the song, no cherry top in the rearview, and our driver is not detained in his quest so this is more like an absence, one humming equally in "Roadrunner" which, already a bit late to notice this, is blessedly free of Johnny Law, maybe that explains a good portion of the song's inner tranquility but let us stay for the moment in 1955, stay in the moment when Chuck Berry first hears the highway sound. In its immediate sense it tells us that the engine quiets as it cools, as engines do, so that he can hear the road around him, highway sound, wind, tires on blacktop, all the things heard in "Once" and "Twice" and "Thrice" and "Physical Speed" and an uncountable host of others, none identical, all the same, or same enough, same because they draw on the same source, not the same song or same musical tradition but the same transformation of the world, a world intricate enough to sustain endless sameness, repetition without tedium.

But he also hears the song just as we do. Maybe the character Maybellene does too and it would be nice to learn of this, but we all hear the same musical break, the same guitar solo, the motor quiets down, the heat cools down, and the highway sound that we hear *is* "Maybellene." Songs are always about themselves even if they don't mean to be, but beyond that truism we can hear the full reach of possibility within "that highway sound." We are—possibly, possibly—listening to a song on the radio wherein someone is listening to the radio. If quieting the motor makes the music audible, we are surely meant to recognize in this the experience of driving along with the radio on, the last element of the rock & roll song, its self-knowledge about its dependence on the radio and especially on the car radio which is finally the real of the highway sound, present from the very beginning, and this is the crucial piece that must be added so as finally to snap together the ur-story, present here as hint and intuition but present nonetheless, part of the whole complex that Berry is trying to figure out on behalf of rock & roll.

Which brings us, finally, to "Johnny B. Goode," the A-side of the single whose B-side is "Around and Around." We began on the ring road and it seems likely we will end there, going around and around, it being peculiarly difficult to escape from such a motion. We have followed the Great Circulator back to where we started, back to 1958 when "Johnny B. Goode" was released, or 1957 when it was recorded, or 1955 when it is said to have been composed. We know already that it goes with "Roadrunner" if for no other reason than that the Sex Pistols, hopelessly and furiously trying to slough off everything that had happened to rock so as to become themselves in 1976, segued in rehearsal from one of these songs to the other, rotten versions both in chronological order, Berry song to Richman song, Johnny's Johnny, Johnny's Jonathan.

Much of the writing about Berry's signature track attends to its singular character, how it is the single rock song that we shot into space, how according to an unsigned *Rolling Stone* entry it is "the first rock & roll hit about rock & roll stardom," how it is Berry's autobiographical moment albeit with "country boy," per the author, swapped in for the first draft's "colored boy," how it features the eloquent description of Johnny's natural gift, how "he could play a guitar just like a-ringin' a bell."

Less commonly mentioned is how that bell also mentioned

near the opening of this chapter persists across Berry's work, is a Berry cliché, how it eventually arrives at Berry's novelty cover "My Ding-a-Ling" with its "silver bells hanging on a string" but is there for the outset: ring! ring! goes the bell. Berry is forever calling us to order so that order can be tested against rock music, the bell is a prolonged summoning we can hear across the span of a career, wake *up*, come *here*, listen to *this*. You hear his bell and start salivating for rock & roll, has there ever been a more Pavlovian artist?

On closer inspection, "Johnny B. Goode" turns out in all its exceptional history to be a Chuck Berry song in general. The Berryness is there in the bell but it is also in the tension between rural and urban life central to the song, a tension that is not a feature of Berry's autobiography but is a feature of the century's turnaround, the tension or opposition between ways of living, ways of working, ways of producing, that is here knit together not by the highway but by railroad tracks. There is a history there, as Kristin Ross reminds us, one tied up in the emergence of modern economies: "The train coincided with a qualitative change in the production/circulation complex in part by bringing a new level of speed to the circulation of goods. Circulation increases the commodity character of goods with a rapidity that is in direct proportion to the physical rapidity of vehicles."[14] She is perilously close to saying "physical speed." What commodity does this train bear? That question goes to the heart of the mystery. The song begins "way back up in the woods among the evergreens" and arrives, at least imaginatively, at a concert venue downtown where Johnny's name is in lights. But to make it from one to the other, to become Johnny B. Goode, Johnny must be discovered, must carry his guitar down to the tracks so that both the train's engineer and "people passing by"—who must be passengers, there is no other possibility—can hear him play and then bear the news of his talents to the city at the end of the line.

Is this not an impossible fantasy? I do not mean the grand fantasy that animates the song wherein an artist is simply discovered, is granted fame by a phalanx of fairy godmothers in the guises of promoters and scouts and schemers. It is easy and sensible to dismiss such stories as false promises of class mobility in allegorical form. And no doubt such events recede once a cultural sector becomes industrialized, begins to function after the fashion of star-maker machinery. But in the early hours of rock & roll, such an event seems plausible enough if not altogether joyous: one need only consider impresario Alan Freed, the New York disc jockey who helped break "Maybellene" and mysteriously ended up with a writing credit on the song. So let us grant that such "discovery" exists largely to the extent that it refers to a kind of persistently racialized theft, a somewhat different allegory, not so much of class mobility but colonial nation making. This surrounds Chuck Berry, as it surrounds Big Mama Thornton and Fred Parris, but it is not the impossible fantasy at the center of "Johnny B. Goode," which concerns a far more local matter: How the fuck does anybody hear an acoustic guitar strummed by some kid leaning back against a tree *from a passing train*??

They don't, is the answer. Trees can't be too close to tracks is one problem but distance is not the primary issue here. Have you ever heard a train? Trains are loud at any speed and in any era, ambiently loud, speed, wind, steel wheels on steel rails, everything is drowned out by that railroad sound. It can't be real, which is to say, it is the part of the story that tells you it is a dream, a displacement between reality and desire, where two narratives that cannot go together are nonetheless aligned. The lyric, taken literally, is set in the prerock era, it cannot be otherwise in that it narrates not just the world's discovery of Johnny but Johnny's of rock & roll and there is your autobiography, there is your doubled origin story. Because it is Before Rock, there cannot be a highway and a car and a radio gathered together. Except that there must be, for the song means also to be rock's ur-story and that means it must include that highway sound. The paradox of genre making again. The song sets out to solve this problem, in the place of a highway and a car and a radio it gives us a railroad line and a train and a live performer playing a song that can somehow be heard *as if* we were driving around listening to the radio in a car, that is the song's great magic trick. And what do we hear?

We hear the same thing the driver hears in "Maybellene." We hear Chuck Berry singing and playing guitar.

But "Johnny B. Goode" is not simply *like* "Maybellene." It means to summon that song without saying its name. The substitution of "country boy" for "colored boy" was no doubt made, as claimed, with an eye toward market viability; at the same time, it cannot help but be a restatement of the Bob Wills / Chuck Berry relation-ship. What's more, Johnny is "strummin' with the rhythm that the drivers made," that plural noun providing the last curious detail. Within the scene conjured by the song it can only refer to the train's drivers and still it solicits us to imagine motorists rolling past. It asks us to hear the guitar, through this elaborate series of displacements, picking out a sound that can accord with the rush of vehicles across the landscape, rolling along the paths that knit together country and city, and now the ur-story is all there, a version of it, we have even that seemingly curious but in truth recurrent character of the fan-become-artist, the ama-teur who, adjacent to the radio, now begins to sing, who in this fucked-up telling *becomes* the radio heard by the passengers. The song is almost too pure in its condensation of things. And we have no choice but to believe that our hero is strumming not just any song but his very first, it's an origin story after all, he must be playing the song that first derives rock & roll from that high-way sound, the song that can't be named because in the narrative timeline imagined by "Johnny B. Goode" no one knows it yet. This is the secret at the exact center of the song, the one that elicits all the surrounding curiosities. "Johnny B. Goode" is a song about hearing the song "Maybellene." The bell is there from the very beginning, right there in the middle syllable!

A provisional summing is in order. A genre has a genealogy insofar as its elements are handed down from tradition, chang-ing along the way, but it cannot be reduced to this genealogy. It is the gathering of these elements into a new arrangement, one that can sing a new configuration of history, of social life. The elements can be discerned in the past but they will not have had the same meanings then as the meanings bestowed upon them by the ensuing transformations of the world. There are sounds and there are highways and yet there is no highway sound, until there is. This means that a genre both does and does not have an origin, that the ur-story must be present at its own birth, like something out of a dream, exactly the dream of "Johnny B. Goode."

"Roadrunner" in its prosaic wakefulness is exactly not a dream. Still, we find ourselves within the loop of the ur-story, in a song listening to a song, all of it provisioned by the same ensemble of elements that we have now reduced to "the highway sound." Let's just say it: the highway sound is "Maybellene" on the radio in Jonathan Richman's car. "Roadrunner" is infinitely in debt to that moment of origin, from which springs both *faster miles an hour* and *radio on*. But it is too late for origins. The night is new, the world is new enough if you're a teenager, but "Roadrunner," for all its newness, its strangeness, its naivete real or contrived (just a hair's breadth between them), does not drive through an origin but an ending, not the end of rock & roll, also a rube's game, but the end of the ensemble that rock & roll birthed itself to sing. It drives through the moment when the ur-story realizes itself so completely that it has to give up the ghost, say farewell to the spirit of 1956.

When we make it back to 1972, ghostly to us now, the system is breaking down. Chuck Berry's v8 Ford chugs into the twilight of post-Fordism from which no rain can rescue it. In Ohio, the Lordstown Assembly Complex sees arguably the last great militant strike by autoworkers, which will end in union compliance and intensified pushes toward automation. The churn of postwar growth is slowing, profits are about to tank, the dispensation that we will call by the uninspired name of "deindustrialization" wheels into view. "By the early 1970s saturation points had been reached in both the domestic and world markets for motorcars," notes a standard history; around this moment, Los Angeles is discovered to have more cars than people.[15] All of this is held within "Roadrunner," the song finds itself in the neighborhood where the American Industrial Revolution began and drives through its ending, drives through a landscape run down, exhausted, just in the midst of becoming quaint, a consumption corridor which is the residue of the production boom that it will survive but only for a while, a magic moment but a bleak magic, that is the song's pathos. Already the neon signs on Route 128 are from an ancient world, echoes across time of Johnny's name in lights. There is nothing to do out there. There is no future, surely this is what allows for a song that offers a present of such sublimity. If rock & roll depends on the fantasy that the joy of riding can be detached from the misery of work, even the miserable work of being a rock & roll star, "Roadrunner" pushes that fantasy to breaking. Maybe it is a dream after all, the dream of pure circulation, driving around and around, no particular place to go for real this time, the ring road finally unstuck from the factory bell.

▶ 04 The Main Streets and the Cinema Aisles, 1997

AND SO WE FIND OURSELVES in 1972 again and then just another mile marker into 1973, from the ascent to the decline of the American epoch, modernity to postmodernity, industrial to finance capital. There's a red thread that runs from 1973 through 1979's conservative counterrevolution, when the ad hoc addresses to national economic decline begin to be systematized, a coordinated arrangement that will be known in the United States as the Reagan Revolution, in the United Kingdom as Thatcherism, and more broadly as "neoliberalism." You will notice the similarity immediately, the way that political-economic dispensations work like musical genres, there's no single thing that makes them, the parts must be brought together in an ensemble elaborated enough that it can become reasonably stable, that it can survive and remake itself over and over even if one or two of the elements are missing. Though "stable" may get matters wrong. Once things start to fall apart for the American juggernaut it is crisis after crisis. The bankruptcy of New York happens in there somewhere, and punk rock.

The red thread runs through to 1989, year of the "Washington Consensus," when the collapse of the Second World briefly promises a respite from the narrative of decline. That same thread runs through 1997–98 when the global fuckup known as the Asian Financial Crisis or Asian Currency Crisis or by the altogether sketchier name of the Asian flu, a name meant to underscore the figure of contagion but also not a little bit racist, spreads from Thailand to Malaysia to Singapore, the Philippines, Indonesia, Hong Kong, South Korea, Russia, Brazil, Argentina, currencies devaluing and defaulting and coming under attack at each stop along the way, and landing on U.S. shores with the collapse of Long-Term Capital Management (LTCM), a hedge fund so heavy that it has to be bailed out to stem the global crisis, or so we're told. The Fed gathered together bankers from more than a dozen gilded and august institutions, for the executive of the modern state is nothing but a committee for managing the common affairs of the whole bourgeoisie, and hurled $3.65 billion at LTCM to deal with its debts on the premise that if it couldn't pay its markers, a series of international financial houses would drop like dominoes. It was at the time the biggest bailout of a private firm in history. Just wait.

Long-Term Capital Management was founded by the guys who developed the mathematical model that made the trading of *non-stuff* a trillion-dollar market. Derivatives, mutual funds, arbitrage, the whole sea change known as "financialization": these guys brought that to life. I mean, it was coming to life anyway, because that is what happens when a massive industrial economy goes into decline, when the real expansion of factories and jobs passes its peak and starts to contract, then it is only finance that can expand along with the other speculative arts, real estate, insurance. But this expansion is fictive, temporary, finally just a reallocation of value from here to there that produces nothing new along the way. Economists, the good ones, think of this as a kind of circulation. They quite often liken it to musical chairs, another figure of music and going around, it's impossible to avoid really, and as long as the increasingly risky speculation continues it looks like a dance until something goes wrong, the music stops, and somebody crashes to the floor. It is a kind of circulation new to this book but not to history. The period after 1973, after "Roadrunner," is not the first time a global economic center undergoes such a shift, for example it happened to the British Empire too, beginning something like a century before, so much so that by 1922, an immigrant poet would describe the capital of London, once shrouded in coal smoke and brutally vibrant, as being "like a little bookkeeper grown old."[1]

So finance was coming, it's how the penthouse predators keep the profits moving, keep the mass of money both real and virtual whirling around, but the question of how best to make it whirl, most swiftly, most advantageously, that is the kind of thing that will call new technologies into being, technologies of the great circulation. That is where LTCM comes in. Its financial tech was the best, everybody believed it, two of the founders would eventually get Nobels for having engineered the best financial tech ever and the third engineer would have gotten one as well but he was dead. The tech was called the Black-Scholes Equation, which for the first time allowed plausible pricing in the present of what a financial instrument would be worth later on, moving gracefully backward and forward in time. The equation zeroed out all the variables except variability itself, zeroed out everything but volatility, and if that is not an image of the future I do not know what is, and this happened just as the profits from industry were drying up so the capital available to the big funds and huge institutions and the hyperwealthy began to slosh into the derivative markets until it was a torrent: that is financialization. So thanks Black-Scholes, a mechanism so powerful that economic historians have called it an "epistemological rupture." It was published in 1973, so maybe it's not a red thread but a ring road that runs through history, moving gracefully backward and forward in time, though out on the ring road it can be hard to tell the difference, going forward means forever curving toward the past, going around and around.

None of this is to argue for something like just deserts, or karma, or other moralizing ideas of the *what-comes-around-goes-around* variety. This is just to name a fact about circulation. When you build the ring road, or the global economy, it becomes possible that something tossed out into the traffic will come back your way again, almost unrecognizable, monstrous, beautiful, who knows? In fact it becomes increasingly likely that this will happen, because the circuits are more closely connected, what the banky boys call *correlation*, all of it faster, less regulated, the kind of thing that makes the free-markets-equal-freedom jocks stain their khakis, and if you toss something catchy out there it's coming back around like the Roadrunner. It feels like freedom but it cuts both ways, sometimes it's the freedom of Jonathan going around and around in his car, and sometimes the Asian flu going around and around in the markets annihilating the lives of Average Joes and Jolenes around the globe while the quants try to figure out how to bet on how bad it will be. And "Roadrunner" itself is not just wheeling through its chord changes but through global culture, two, three, many Roadrunners, it circulates through the relays of Greg Kihn and the Sex Pistols, circulates through Buzzcocks, who are probably the poppiest band to come out of the Manchester Free Trade Hall show on June 4, 1976, and who used to soundcheck with the song, it circulates through the Feelies and Yo La Tengo and Joan Jett's quick and holy version. Around and around goes the song and inevitably something really interesting happens: it lands on the second track of an album by a British South Asian band except it's a little hard to recognize because it has different words and a different melody and it isn't about the radio and Massachusetts but about vinyl 45s and playback singers and especially Asha Bhosle, the most renowned and revered of playback singers, who recorded more than twelve thousand songs for Bollywood cinema.

For all these reasons it's a little hard at first to hear that "Brimful of Asha" is Tjinder Singh's version of "Roadrunner" come back around as a global idea. It's a little hard to hear because "Asha" asks us to hear a good deal else, from the Punjabi invocation that opens the album version to the roll call of beloved musical artists to the repetitive fade with its one-line chorus, "brimful of Asha on the forty-five," as well as "everybody needs a bosom for a pillow" repeated right up until the abrupt final phrase, "mine's only forty-five." Can we visualize the brimful in question? Not with any great certainty. Perhaps we are meant to understand that the seven-inch as seen from above, spinning in Singh's room or in his memory, is like a cup brimming with the sound of Asha Bhosle. Perhaps we are meant to see the vinyl platter as a hat brim, similarly filled. It is not so much that it is ambiguous but that it is figurative language of a sort that recurs throughout the song, enough to locate the lyrics in a distinct category from "Roadrunner," at a distance from Richman's insistence on direct speech, literal description, the *thisness* of its objects. Of course he has "faster miles an hour" and "modern moonlight," to be impeccably literal is almost impossible, but the difference is clear enough and so it is at first a little hard to hear that they are the same song.

"There's dancing behind movie scenes, behind the movie scenes, *Sadi Rani*," it opens after the invocation, shortly transforming "movie scenes" to "movie screens" by which point the world conjured by the song is more or less in place, the world as soundstage with a seventy-seven-thousand-piece orchestra set, the world as movie, as sound + image, the romantic leads pushed up close to us, behind them the elaborate collective dance that typifies the Bollywood musical, all of this on the screen with its counterfeit of the third dimension. And behind the screen, behind the scene, Asha Bhosle, *Sadi Rani*, Our Queen.

Playback singers occupy an ambiguous position in Bollywood, distinct both from Hollywood's song-and-dance stars and from soundtrack heroes. They voice the songs that the stars seem to sing. On the one hand, industrial habit maintains the casual fiction of performance: reviews regularly identify a song with the actor, essays on films often do not mention the singers at all while carefully detailing screenwriters, music directors, and so on. On the other hand, there is no official secrecy as one sometimes encounters in Hollywood. Successful playback singers are known to all the audiences found along the main streets and the cinema aisles. The tension resides in the term "playback," which gets at something specific not to Bollywood's musical production process but to its cinematic production process more broadly. The industry for a very long time, into the nineties, used exclusively non-sync recording such that the dialogue would be dubbed in later by the actors, the same actors charged with matching the songs that would be played back while filming, and so for a very long time, there is never a "natural" moment where sound and image are truly simultaneous and everyone knows it, it's artifice all the way down.

This anxiety about nature and artifice has been at the heart of cinema's self-knowledge ever since talkies arrived. It's the thing movies can't stop thinking about, or maybe it's the atmosphere surrounding all movies, maybe it's just the weather, like the rain that provides the setting for an implausible percentage of Bollywood songs, and surely you saw this coming, the rain like *Singin' in the Rain*, Hollywood's own soundstaging of this exact problem of who is singing when, of who is a real singer. At the climax, Lina Lamont is compelled to perform live at the premier of the film within the film, *The Dancing Cavalier*, and because she cannot *really* sing (well in truth the underlying issue is that she sounds like a working-class person putting on airs, but that is another matter, a different Hollywood autobiography, that popular entertainment trying to pass itself off as art), Cathy Selden stands behind the curtain and sings for Lina, a perfect execution of musical dubbing done live, or so goes the film's conceit, and of course for this moment of perfect playback singing in real time they perform the title song. The deception would work if our male leads backstage did not hoist the curtain and give the game away, expose the fact that there's singing behind the movie screen, cue laughter, then tears, then a kiss, though as this is a movie within a movie the artifice is never truly exposed, just kicked to a higher level.

Hollywood can only offer imperfect allegories for Bollywood, in no small part because of different production practices much less the different social histories in which they take form. Bollywood's logic of universal dubbing means that all compiling of sound + image must be understood as collaboration to make a scene rather than competition for primacy. Asha Bhosle is not at war with Zeenat Aman, who helps picturize Bhosle's great hit "Chura Liya Hai Tumne Jo Dil Ko" from *Yaadon Ki Baaraat* (1973, shocker), the way that Cathy Selden is at war with Lina Lamont. The image from *Singin' in the Rain* nonetheless offers a couple of ways to think about playback singers, about what is pushed out front and what is behind, about what is solid and what is for want of a better word liquid, and finally about the transformation of the world to which this book keeps returning.

That image of the playback singer standing there behind a curtain, a literalization of the production process, a *picturization* (as Bollywood texts have it) of a thousand playback singers standing behind a thousand movie screens, is yet another gloss on our ur-story. Playback singers are in evident ways the opposite of the amateurs found in "Song of the Kite" and in "Johnny B. Goode," found in the person of Jonathan Richman in and around 1972; indeed, they are singers of such professionalism that they vanish into the songs, the films, the scenes. And yet that invisibility is the link. They are not *quite* in the place of the music but instead, like Cathy Selden, they are somehow *adjacent*, that crucial term in the ur-story: next to the radio, next to the song. There is Lina

Lamont, the star, singing into the ostentatious microphone for all the dishonest world to see. There in similar fashion is all of Bollywood's on-screen talent crooning or purring or belting it out in the middle of a movie scene—and behind the movie screen, adjacent to the music and yet in the end the music's true source, is the playback singer.

But the larger sense of "behind" is perhaps more helpful here, in the sense of what makes it all happen, the *driving force* in the sense provided by the Punjabi invocation that opens "Brimful," translated as "Our hope remains with us like a driving force day and night in both good and bad times." It is not exactly our hope that makes it all happen so much as the singers, and in Punjabi, hope is *Asha*. In defiance of the Western genre system (which, despite the proliferation of crosstalk and outright theft among national traditions, offers an impoverished framework through which to view other cinemas), Bollywood films are almost without fail punctuated by scenes in which characters sing and dance. Perhaps this means they are all musicals, though perhaps if all films are musicals then no films are, any more than a night out with your friends, inevitably involving songs on the car radio or at karaoke or in the living room, is a musical. Or maybe that means that all life is a musical.

In any regard, the musical sequences are, perhaps more than any other aspect of the films, what makes the industry work. Within the discontinuous production process of Bollywood, the musical numbers are often produced early on and used as decisive fundraising and publicity vehicles toward completion of the films, and the songs will frequently generate a core portion of revenues; they dominate the pop charts and the classics stations and enter deeply into the social fabric, serving as "part of wedding processions, election rallies, and religious festivals; they blare from cassette players in tea stalls and from speakers in taxis and auto-rickshaws."[2] The playback artist is the half-secret singer behind everything, assuring "the central place of cinema in moral, aesthetic, developmentalist, and modernization discourses about Indian society." Maybe that is what is meant by keeping the dream alive.[3] And cinema in turn can play this role, can sit firmly at the center of a story about the nation, exactly because of its ability, carried forth by song, to leave that nation behind, to circle the planet: "Cinema's significance in a neoliberal economic imaginary arises, however, from its ability to circulate in a variety of global markets, which becomes a cause for nationalist celebrations."[4]

We have come a long way from "Roadrunner," from in and around 1972. But maybe in some sense that attenuation is the pleasure, this following of links or steps, skein of connection, what is set next to which, this concatenation of songs and moments, maybe that is part of what pop means, and part of what fandom means, and part of what scholarship means, and certainly part of what circulation means, and the wider the curve the more it takes in until it is fully global, the circuit set at maximum, culture like a ring of Saturn cinched around the planet, which on closer inspection turns out as ever to be an innumerable number of rocks whirling around together except it isn't just culture, that is what I have been trying to figure out, it is the economic and the political and the cultural, not so easily separable, forming one big circuit.

And lo, this running together of the economic and the political and the cultural turns out to be the song's concern as it arrives, having lingered over movies and music, at its third verse. "And singing, illuminate the main streets and the cinema aisles," it begins, an ambiguous parallelism, we see the similarity of the images immediately but are the streets in the films or are they beyond the theater exits? Are we reminded that when we leave the movie house we have not left the world lit by song? Perhaps like the song's construction, pursued through a tissue of allusion, this is a textbook example of what we were once in the habit of calling postmodernism, that great theorization of the epoch, of its liquid character, its collapse of the so-called representational and the so-called real into a single level, the endlessly expanding plane of signification, the world of artifice and the artificing of the world, simulation blah blah blah, and surely who could make a hard distinction between main streets and cinema aisles when the Disney Corporation had broken ground on the town of Celebration, Florida, in 1996? At least the song finally has a road to run.

Or a road to ruin. The very next thing that happens is, "We don't care about no government warning, about that promotion of the simple life and the dams they're building," and with great suddenness we are asked to recognize the distance between the confines of the cinema featuring the sweep of Asha Bhosle's fluent soprano and the existence of, say, the largest construction project of India's history: the mass production of hydroelectric structures conceived in the fifties but begun in earnest in the seventies and scaling up massively in the nineties, those building blocks of globalization tearing India apart. Singh likely has in mind the Sardar Sarovar Dam, the one that will shortly be taken up by Arundhati Roy in "The Greater Common Good" as she makes her famous turn from fiction to political essays, representation to real again.

The dam was the largest of thirty in the Narmada Valley Project and thus the one that met with the broadest and most sustained opposition from the impoverished residents of the valley and beyond starting in the late eighties and taking on force in the years just before "Asha," a confrontation between local existence and global capital. The dams were among other things mandated by the International Monetary Fund (IMF), which along with the World Bank would provide the Indian state with desperately needed loans on condition of currency devaluation, deregulation, privatization, which is to say, the very model of a structural adjustment program through which the wealthiest nations capture the energies of, say, former colonies, drawing Indian wealth and resources into the transnational circuits, assuring the imposition of capital-friendly austerity at home. "Since 1991," notes Tejaswini Ganti, "state economic policy has increasingly catered to and focused on urban, middle-class consumers, to the detriment of the majority of Indian society who have no use for commodities such as automobiles, cosmetics, electronics, household appliances, and soft drinks when their basic needs of food, water, sanitation, shelter, primary education, and healthcare have not been met."[5] For that majority, including the millions displaced by the dam projects, the prizes of what we like to call modernity will not be on offer. In its place, the government's promotion of the simple life, an ennobling name for misery if there ever was one and the song knows it. But we don't care about any of this, it insists immediately, with an implausible or maybe just aspirational account of music's power, because we have a brimful of Asha.

To peer at the span from "Roadrunner" to "Brimful of Asha," from the rise of dam planning in India to the frenzy of dam building, from the global financial crisis of 1973 to the global financial crisis of 1997–98, is to peer at a peculiar epoch. I mean, they are all peculiar epochs. And it is worth saying again that we are really talking about three different epochs: one for anglophone pop music and the Western histories within which it arises; another for the cultural and political-economic trajectory of India; and a third epoch unfolding at the level of what we might call the global macro, which by the way is also the name of a particular investment strategy most famously employed by George Soros during the Asian Financial Crisis and involving hardcore currency speculation as national economies collapsed. These epochs happen at the same time but are not the same and there are risks in comparison or analogy especially between the first two, but then there is the way that the third, the global macro, keeps drawing aspects of the others into its circuits and drawing its energies from them and shaping them in return, this is another secret of the great circulation. If it doesn't render a total homogeneity across the surface of the planet, it does at least mean that everything exchanges, even things that are incommensurate and incomparable, it means that the driving forces in one place can shape matters in another, that if something form-giving happens somewhere, this process starts to happen everywhere and it moves faster and faster as the circuits are drawn tight.

This is in part just to say what has happened, what happens between the two songs, the distance of separation by a quarter century, the nearness of sharing the same ring road. Tjinder Singh, born in Wolverhampton to a father who had been relocated by Indian Partition, founds Cornershop in 1991, the name ironizing the stereotype of convenience stores having British South Asian proprietors, not so different from the California stereotype of the Korean-owned market that would play a fatal role during the L.A. Riots of 1992, the same year that Cornershop burns a poster of Morrissey outside the offices of his label EMI in protest against his flag-shrouded performances of nationalist racism. This too is part of the song's prehistory.

"Asha" hews more closely to the conventions of the popular song form than "Roadrunner": intro, three loose verses with choruses following. All is dispatched within about two minutes, leaving three minutes in the original version for exactly what you would be waiting for if you were tuning in for the afterlife of "Roadrunner": a list, pleasures spooling past, going around and around, this time circling not on the highway but on the platter, two ring roads if there ever was one. Maybe it's just a bridge, but the song makes it last. The list is a way of making a record. Each time Singh calls out a name, the band responds "forty-five" and the record keeps spinning, keeps coming back around. The song lists Mohamed Rafi and Lata Mangeshkar, two more Bollywood titans (the latter being Bhosle's sister), lists Jacques Dutronc and the Bolan Boogie, France, England, lists "Bancs Publics," the George Brassens song with its cinematic image of lovers on park benches, Paris, everywhere.

The mixture of this list echoes or colludes with the song's setting of Punjabi in advance of English. Singh has discussed this syncretism in the language of composition, saying, "I see it as a sort of sampling, another texture, another layer."[6] Within the dynamic set loose in "Asha," it becomes as well a story of cultural circulation itself, of how pop was global as soon as you could easily move a song from here to there. It proposes that the transnational whirl levels everything out, that it allows for an antiracist orbit wherein the glories of the former colony are not subordinated to those of empire, borders are permeable, things exchange equally in a way that promises more than formal equality. The figures, the sounds, the powers do not congeal into hierarchy because they will not be allowed to stop moving, the single keeps moving, that's the thing, it will keep passing through you even when you yourself are still, having already passed through a series of media.

This is an optimistic view of culture. We know that it comes with its other, that concrete form of cultural circulation that can never float free from its origins in colonization. Punjabi culture comes to one of those West Midlands towns featuring a hundred bicycle makers and a bowling green first via transnational migration, which looks like freedom only from a great distance and up close always turns out to be crop failure, political persecution, labor markets, infrastructural neglect, civil war, the assorted refluxes of empire. It would be implausible to tell the story of global circulation without placing migration at the center alongside global finance, one the movement of people harried and held up at every border, one the whoosh of capital which will not be detained even for an instant. This human circulation will return in the next chapter; it is never absent. Cultural circulation in some degree serves the exact function concealing this truth, serving to render the hope and misery of populations set in motion, the loss and risk of it, as something frictionless and shareable and even joyous. That is the song's optimism and perhaps it is an empty optimism, much like the implausible unconcern of "we don't care about the dams they're building," claims that are obviously false and nonetheless true to the sense of what music can provide, at least for a few minutes. And we need not believe these claims, or even believe that the song believes them, to understand the ways that such ideas might be compelling to a lover of music, particularly one trying to make their way through the thicket of multiple, overlapping cultures.

Such a vision of flows premised in cultural exchangeability is also, and this seems important, the opposite of the dams, which are premised entirely on power unevenly distributed, on imbalances nationally and globally, on hierarchies running from the caste and class systems to the international divisions of labor and resources. Transnational pop versus transnational power. What after all is a dam but the fact and figure of blockage? A dam promises the power that comes from stopping things, from motion interrupted. Is this not like the mysterious wall in the previous chapter the exact negative of the ring road, of spinning vinyl, of the song going around and around, of a sort of anti-dam? The song is complicated in its transfers, liquid, mercurial, but the chords are incorrigibly simple, three chords and three only circling around in a calm and recursive jangle, a shape almost as simple as "Roadrunner," the exact same chords plus one, A/E/D, and Singh also names solid-state radio, *forty-five*, and a specific low-cost brand called the Ferguson Mono, *forty-five*, and the two-in-one radio/cassette player, *forty-five*, and once more we are passing near to the ur-story, it is just what you would expect to encounter out on the ring road: dusty and aging technologies, the disposable commodities that always, named or not, accompany the disposable commodity of the pop song, faded as the labels of forty-fives from Argo Records and Trojan Records, he names them too.

By now it is clear that the song is no more about Asha Bhosle than it is about the single itself, that black vinyl brim—no more about the media figures who provide content for singles than about the media that carry them into a kid's room, no more about playback singers than playback methods. And here things become clear. It is not the playback singer who, in our ur-story, stands in the place of the amateur adjacent to the radio but the kid in the bedroom, the kid made explicit in the video, going around and around amid faded commodities both beautiful and trivial, on the verge of putting them all into a song, circling with the single that is the form that provisions all other forms, a ring road cast in vinyl.

The song is dialectical through and through is what I am trying to say. Reaching outward to throw its arms around the world, the song in the very same gesture turns inward like the groove that the stylus follows around a seven-inch, turns inward to become its own subject. Centrifugal motion, centripetal motion. And then one more reversal: having turned inward, having turned from the transnational circuits into a Wolverhampton bedroom, it lofts our paradigmatic kid into the great circulation.

And like a magic spell Singh's song, single about singles, turns out to be Cornershop's first global hit, a song about global pop but also about the conditions through which global pop hits become possible, the purling of value that keeps passing through us as it circles the planet, the financial circuits helping remake the international order. The song comes out in 1997 but it doesn't really accelerate until the next year, as the Asian flu is spreading to Russia and South America, when the song is remixed by Norman Cook, elsewhere known as Fatboy Slim, and this is surely one of the greatest remixes in history, it brings out the genius of the song without fucking it up, without compromising its scope and minimalism, its ceaseless momentum, its three basic chords, sometimes just two, its way of being about itself and also everything. And at the same time Norman Cook makes a critical reading of the song, the remix is seven and a half minutes long but it wants to show how the song is infinite, a repetitive structure filled with endless possibility from the morning past the evening to the end of the light, he speeds up the homespun jangle more than 10 percent which is a lot, *faster beats per minute*, and more important, he pushes the jangle forward so that the elaborate dance mix nonetheless says *I am the simplest of rock songs, all I want is everything*, and meanwhile Cook pulls items from the list and sets them at the head of the song, sets them throughout, but he also keeps the list intact, he insists that the catalog of artist and apparatus is not the bridge but the whole road, when we arrive at the list, to that point having heard only bits and pieces, he empties out its backing music, for a few moments it is just the singer that he is playing back, and he extends the final breakdown on into the middle of the night until you can hear, it's obvious, that *"forty-five"* is *"radio on"* and that Cornershop is the Postmodern Lovers and the guitar goes around and around and the remix goes to number 1.

▶ 05 World Runner, 2007

SO YOU HAVE THESE SONGS making circular sounds and it turns out they are trying to think about circulation, about records on turntables and cars on ring roads and sounds in the transnational flow of culture: the relaying of sonic contagions through the system and around the globe and often returning to where they began but different, mutated. There's probably no better example than Rihanna's Stargate's Michael Jackson's Quincy Jones's Manu Dibango's "Soul Makossa," which is from everywhere and also Cameroon, from every year and also from 1972, shocker. Influence and pastiche and the import-export business are nothing new but such contagions and mutations intensify and accelerate within the regime of mobile capital that we often call globalization, until they become inseparable from the very idea of pop music: *finance capital pop*, a name that seems at first unfair because finance capital is basically a bunch of glass-office motherfuckers charging rent on money they don't own even as they rocket that money around the planet looking for ruinously fast yields even if it means debasing an entire region or nation or hemisphere, while the songs we are following along the same circuits are lovely and blameless. But that's okay, understanding the elaborate character of this relationship is exactly what we are up to and we are not the only ones. These conditions through which the circulation of sonic cultures becomes possible and inevitable and proceeds at a pace of approximately faster miles an hour are not just the history of pop, they are the history of history, they are conjoined with the development of what we now call "the world-system," and *this*—not what anyone says in a song—is why pop music is political.

So it is only to be expected that some of the most interesting pop musicians would take this as pop's representational problem, the way the nineteenth-century European novel took the urbanizing social order emerging with industrial production as its representational problem, its *formal* problem. And I am telling you that M.I.A. is a great pop artist, not because of the ferocious invention of song after song during the period of her greatness but because this is her project. The same way that we speak of artists and scholars *working on* music or literature or history or dance, M.I.A. works on circulation and she gets around. She's crafty.

But the circulation she pores over is more developed than we have yet confronted, because it is not just the circulation of mobile capital but mobile labor, not quite *as* mobile because as far as capital is concerned, money gotta be free and humans not so much. Just as it was there in "Asha," in the question of how Tjinder Singh's family ended up in Wolverhampton, the matter of migration is everywhere in M.I.A. It's there in the book titled *M.I.A.*, collecting work from her stint at Central Saint Martins School of Art, published just before her music career takes flight. The biographical note, that item whose veracity one never knows quite how much to credit, claims that when she arrived in London with her family of war refugees, she "spoke only two words of English: 'Michael' and 'Jackson.'"[1] *Mama-say, mama-sa, ma-makossa*, that is all ye know on earth, and all ye need to know.

But the theme of global migrancy begins in her biography. M.I.A. is born Mathangi Arulpragasam in London 1975—seven years after Singh's birth, a span in which everything happens, including "Roadrunner"—to Sri Lankan parents who in 1976 move back to Jaffna, center of the nation's Tamil population. More relocations follow, Madras, Jaffna again, and then back to London just before her eleventh birthday, the family living for a while as refugees. In these years, she goes by Maya. These early peregrinations can in many ways be written down to the political affiliations of her father, Arul, most notably as cofounder of the Eelam Revolutionary Organization of Students (EROS) right around the time of Maya's birth, when he also spent some months in Lebanon training with the Fatah wing of the Palestine Liberation Organization (PLO).

Eelam is the Tamil name for Sri Lanka and EROS was adjacent to, but supposedly not part of, the Liberation Tigers of Tamil Eelam (LTTE), the revolutionary army known as the Tamil Tigers, who were formed, hmm, right there in 1976, and who fought the long and brutal civil war that would not end until 2009 when they finally conceded defeat. For a while EROS served as a sort of theoretical cadre for the Tigers, Maya drawing the distinction like this: "The Tigers had machetes and said, 'They killed my mum so I'm going to fucking fight them.' And my dad was like, 'No no no no, read this amazing book about revolution. Let's sit down and draw up a manifesto.'"[2] So there is a certain opacity, and we are never quite sure whether her estranged father has taken up arms or not. That uncertainty—the manifesto or the fight, ideas or arms— haunts the music. We think, *maybe*.

That is backstory. And it will turn out that M.I.A., as Maya starts calling herself around the millennium, everybody gets an acronym in this fight, takes these things as her material. She takes Sri Lanka and its political struggles in particular, and the distinction she wants to draw regarding whether her dad was a pacific intellectual or a Tamil freedom fighter slash terrorist is maybe a little disingenuous since she depends on the drift between cultural forms and political action, she is an artist of that ambiguity, cannot stop intertwining sounds and revolutionary violence like two strands of DNA. The *M.I.A.* volume may cite Michael Jackson and feature a short text by Elastica's Justine Frischman, but the stencilesque street art that it collects returns incessantly to Sri

Lankan militants and soldiers mixed with recurrent images of tigers, sometimes leaping out of grenades. Those are the moving parts. This will run her into all kinds of trouble, trouble for being down with armed struggle, trouble for *not* being down with armed struggle, all the ills that befall the artist who represents militancy for the market, that endlessly self-undermining action.

"Pull Up the People," musical opener on her official 2005 debut, *Arular* (titled for her father's nom de guerre, not a wise decision as security culture goes), offers a stark drum track, and the pre-chorus runs "slang tang, that's the M.I.A. thang." Well, it sounds like she is saying "slang tang," maybe a gesture toward her own argot drawn from global hot zones, slang with a tang, but perhaps it is "sleng teng," the name for one of the most common Jamaican rhythms. Let's say both. We are never in just one place, that's the M.I.A. thing, and then she says, "I got the bombs to make you blow, I got the beats to make you bang." There it is, far from the only example but likely the best, and it is worth noticing that she is not claiming she has bomb beats, everyone says that, but that she has beats *and* bombs, manifesto and machete, sound and the fury, not that one does the work of the other but they go together. Maybe this is a good time to point out that her first mixtape, built on boosted beats, is called, as it must be, *Piracy Funds Terrorism*. It is her way of naming the whole procedure, the whole ambiguity, of saying her own true name. The title "Pull Up the People" no doubt has a thousand references but one of them is surely "serve the people," the slogan offered by Mao—perhaps I should have mentioned the Tigers' affiliation with India's Maoist-inflected Naxalites—and later adopted by the Black Panthers, and bear in mind that the elite LTTE soldiers are called Black Tigers, and all of this is running through the music.

She takes up this political history in particular but in ways that are perhaps less obvious but even more omnipresent she takes up circulation in general. Her case seems to be that it is the basis for pop music. On the very next track of *Arular*, she seems to be talking back to the 1979 song actually called "Pop Muzik," autumnal flower of the disco era. The artist known as M says, "London Paris New York Munich everybody talk about pop muzik," but the artist known as M.I.A. says, "London, quieten down, I need to make a sound. New York, quieten down, I need to make a sound." And then she goes to Kingston and Brazil because her version of circulation escapes the metropoles of the West, that is sort of the point, and along with her producer Diplo she brings in grime, dancehall, Afrobeat, bhangra, baile funk, that's five continents right there. but these aren't her *sounds*, they're what's going around on the big ring road. Her sound is the big ring road itself. She is in no particular place. Her sound is globalization.

But even before then, before *Arular*, when she is a mixtape artist circulating pirated tracks on the internet, her very first single begins, "London calling, speak the slang now," and tosses the hook right into the space of flows and the song starts circling, sinister and joyous, West Indian patois and the chorus-chant going around like jump rope and someone is driving around London and M.I.A. is around London sort of like Tjinder Singh, the song is halfway between "Roadrunner" with its aimless ring road and "Asha" with its global circuit of sounds and people, or maybe it is just Chuck Berry with a whole lot of drugs, "razor blades, galang-a-lang-a-lang, purple haze, galang-a-lang-a-lang," just like ringing a bell.

The song is "Galang" and it seizes fearlessly on the history of music about going around and around, except this time by way of Sri Lanka, and you can hear that too, hear a civil war still ongoing at the time of the song's writing, a civil war that goes around and around, twenty-five years during which the Tamil Tigers, on the rebel side of asymmetrical warfare, perfect the craft of suicide bombing, that canonical form of terrorism that shortly goes around the world like a contagion. They did not invent it, though they are said to have invented the explosive vest, that is who the Black Tigers are. Between 2002 and 2008, suicide bombing increases tenfold globally. The reasons are not complicated. As a leading expert notes with confounding simplicity, "Suicide terrorism is mainly not so much driven by religion, independent of circumstance, but it's mainly a response to foreign military occupation."[3] Tactics and terror circulate like people and finance and culture, and maybe you know that Sri Lanka was once Ceylon and that the war is much older than twenty-five years, that the local is the global, that the island has been divided for centuries and was occupied by the Portuguese and conquered by the United Provinces when they sat at the center of the world system because it was of interest to the Dutch East India Company, and then conquered by the British because it was of interest to their cover version, the British East India Company—what you might call *Double Dutch*—and with their navies behind them, never have the firm and the state been so hard to distinguish. The companies go around and around the blue globe and even though this surely is terror in its most profane avatar we learn to call this geopolitics and eventually via the reflux of empire we come back around to London and *who the hell is hunting you in your BMW* and the song goes around and around, galang-a-lang-a-lang. It is a frightening song and the M.I.A. era has begun. For about five years, she will make the greatest music of the new millennium. It is 2003.

The year 2003 matters, and by now you know the pattern: 2003 matters because of the reemergence of influenza A virus subtype H5N1. I say "reemergence" because it first leapt from waterfowl to humans, killing six in Hong Kong, in 1997, the year of "Asha" and the so-called Asian flu. The H5N1 virus is often called "avian influenza," or more commonly, "bird flu." Among many contagions, contagion itself.

Bird flu is pure pop; it goes around the world. In 2004 Shigeru Omi, regional director of the World Health Organization, forecast "at least seven million deaths, but maybe more—10 million, 20 million, and in the worst case, 100 million." This is perhaps the most predictable of epidemics, predictable because we built the situation ourselves. "Human-induced environmental shocks—

overseas tourism, wetland destruction, a corporate 'Livestock Revolution,' and the Third World urbanization with the attendant growth of megaslums—are responsible for turning influenza's extraordinary Darwinian mutability into one of the most dangerous biological forces on our besieged planet," notes Mike Davis in his 2005 book *The Monster at Our Door: The Global Threat of Avian Flu*, which will itself be counted as prediction when it is republished with due haste and a new epilogue fifteen years later in the face of a global pandemic following much the same course, the novel coronavirus known as COVID-19.[4] That one leaps first not from birds but bats. If you stay alive long enough you come to suspect that everything comes around again, changed just enough that you can call the unspooling years history, old themes and new mutations, a single strand of RNA but different this time. Sitting here in the lost spring of 2020, I am finishing this book from a quarantine that Shigeru Omi and Mike Davis saw coming, and maybe M.I.A.

Among the environmental shocks he lists, Davis puts special emphasis on the last, on the population realignment that has the effect of "shifting the burden of global poverty from the countryside to the slum peripheries of new megacities. Ninety-five percent of future world population growth will be in the poor cities of the South, with immense consequences for the ecology of disease."[5] These are the zones of contagion, artificial hells left by capital's promise of paradise, by the destruction of agrarian life, people driven from their land and into the catchments of the great

cities that cannot sustain them, forced into precarious economies without security or services, progress in all its catastrophe.
These zones will occupy Davis in his next book, *Planet of Slums*,
the shantytowns built up around Lagos and Bogotá, Mumbai and
Mexico City, the favelas of São Paulo that gave life to baile funk.
There are world cities, and then there are the world towns that
encircle them like the ring roads along whose courses they regularly condense. When M.I.A. makes her circumnavigation, she
passes through these towns, their condition captured by Davis's
subtitle, *Urban Involution and the Informal Working Class*—filled
with the floating, the latent, the stagnant surplus populations,
not surplus to our sense of humanity but, more fatally, superfluous to the profit-making machinery, bearers of economist
Joan Robinson's truth that "the misery of being exploited by capi-
talists is nothing compared to the misery of not being exploited
at all."[6] They are the end point of the disposable commodity we
have been following all along, used up and discarded or never
even used, born as remnants.

From *Piracy Funds Terrorism* through *Arular* and 2007's *Kala*
(named after her mom, naturally), M.I.A. fashions something
like the soundtrack to *Planet of Slums*, or maybe simpler just
to say it is the soundtrack to surplus populations. The music is
a riot, dense and anxious, the blister and bang of places treated
as wastelands but waiting to blow. At the far end of the span,
she makes a song that works as a landing spot for this arc of her
music. It is called "World Town." It takes off fast with another

playground chant, hand claps going anarchic, a sort of siren that is maybe like balloons rubbed one against the other punctuated by cartridge click, echoes of Bomb Squad production style, Public Enemy at global scale, fear of a bleak planet. "See me see me bubbling quietly," she says but that can't last and sure enough things turn as anthemic as M.I.A. will get, "hands up, guns out, represent now world town." The ambiguity built into the hip-hop slang usage of *represent* is never more intense: appear, show us what you're made of, both of them, absolutely imperative. The song is a wish image, a revenge fantasy on behalf of the towns left out of the global circulation, no that's not quite right, they may be left out but remain under its sway, it passes through them, it decides who is included and who is pushed out to the ring road as planetary surplus, who is left to hustle in the places where particularity fights a losing battle against the role of the relay, the situation in which contagions circulate.

It is this that loops through the song on *Kala* called "Bird Flu," the loop self-produced and disturbing, mesmerizing and comparable to nothing in pop music except maybe the gurgling baby loop made for Aaliyah in "Are You That Somebody?" It's an ominous bird squawk against an even more ominous clatter of drums, but it's also the whole situation of pop music, in which cars and sounds and economic disasters and pandemics circulate, and the song is terrifying like pop songs rarely songs go out of their way to be. If "Gimme Shelter" is the bad vibes of the failed project called the sixties, the bad vibes of "Bird Flu" are more articulated and nonetheless broader in their sweep, and the failure it calls up is both more recent and more long-standing.

It is very hard to say where bird flu comes from. The 2003 outbreak isolated in Hong Kong flared a month earlier in China, where "the WHO office in Beijing received an email warning that 'a strange contagious disease' had killed more than a hundred people in Guangdong in a single week."[7] Severe Acute Respiratory Syndrome (SARS), a novel coronavirus yet closer to COVID-19, emerged in the same region, China's industrial hub, in 2002. No one is surprised that the hyperdevelopment of South China might prove an incubator for a pandemic. But the driver of the "Livestock Revolution" is Tyson Foods, which kills 2.2 billion chickens annually and is "globally synonymous with scaled-up, vertically integrated production; exploitation of contract growers; visceral antiunionism; rampant industrial injury; downstream environmental dumping; and political corruption."[8] The Legos of late capitalism, Tyson Foods is Global Fried Chicken with an Arkansas accent. When bird flu arrives in Little Rock, it will be very hard to say it came from somewhere else.

As it happens, there is a single effective treatment for avian influenza: trade name Tamiflu. As of *Kala* there was not very much of it; the patent holder, Gilead Sciences, had historically gone to great lengths to prevent its inexpensive reproduction in the world towns. Between George W. Bush's inauguration and 2007, which is to say, more or less between "Galang" and "Bird Flu," Gilead stock increased in value by more than 800 percent.

And as it also happens, the former corporate chairman and still major stakeholder of Gilead is also signatory to the Magna Carta of the Washington Consensus, the "Statement of Principles" of the Project for a New American Century. That document is not equal to the least M.I.A. song but it is far more bellicose, largely concerning the need for a prolonged terror regime to preserve global wealth disparities favoring the United States. This is the tune George Kennan whistled back at the outset of the Long Boom, a song of the past now coughed up again amid what everybody knows is long decline. Nothing is more chilling than the innocuously phrased bullet point 4, "We need to accept responsibility for America's unique role in preserving and extending an international order friendly to our security, our prosperity, and our principles."[9] That is how the managing committee for the bourgeoisie pronounces hellfire from above. The document, no surprise here, dates to 1997, and here we remember not only Cornershop but also the financial crisis that rippled out from Asia to menace every market on the planet. The former Gilead chair is Donald Rumsfeld; you may know him as an apostle of the War on Terror. And M.I.A. writes, "I CALLED THIS BIRD FLU BECAUSE THIS BEAT GON KILL EVERYONE!!"

So this is one thing you can say about *Kala*: M.I.A. is talking to Donald Rumsfeld. They are talking about bird flu and asymmetrical warfare, they are talking about circulation and contagion and global finance. They are talking about blowback and chickens coming home to roost and welcome to the terrorflu. And the conversation circles the globe, but it doesn't begin in some war zone or some necrojungle but on Route 128 when it's late at night. "Bird Flu" is the second track on the disc but before that comes opening track "Bamboo Banga." Let's say the song is a mission statement, and early on in that song, first verse, she lists "Somalia, Angola, Ghana Ghana Ghana," the last spoken thrice like a magic spell, the first African nation to gain independence in the wave of decolonization beginning in the fifties. It's a Bandung banga. And then she lists "India, Sri Lanka, Burma bamboo banga," possibly having in mind the "bamboo curtain" that once demarcated Asia's communist bloc from the rest of the continent and as of 2007 simply designated the isolation of, sure enough, Burma, or Myanmar as M.I.A. pointedly does not call it. Another endless civil war. In any regard, we are back in the world towns. It's a jungle banger, a cold jammer, she says so.

But even before the first verse there is an intro, finally by traveling in reverse we have arrived at the very beginning of the song at the very beginning of the album, the whole package starts with nine seconds of drums and her first words are "Roadrunner Roadrunner, going hundred miles per hour." Now there is an invocation. But the speed is dialed down—remember "At more than a hundred miles an hour, there's a presumption of eternity"?—to exactly the limit that divides eternity from just driving fast. She dedramatizes the situation a bit because after all she already has a civil war and a whole lot more, and she repeats the invocation before adding, "with your radio on, *with your radio on,*" and then runs through the whole thing again, speeding through the world towns, we can assume she's listening to Modern Lovers just like we suspect that Jonathan was listening to Chuck Berry except the beat is from a Tamil movie soundtrack: "Bamboo Banga" is credited to M.I.A. and her writing partner Switch but it is also credited to Jonathan Richman and lastly to Ilaiyaraaja, a prolific Indian film composer whose songs tend to be very difficult to sing and as a result have fallen to the best playback singers, foremost among them Asha Bhosle. *Forty-five.* Small world. No, it's a big world but M.I.A. gets around, everything gets around, because we have built the world that way.

We can say the route from Berry to Richman to Cornershop to M.I.A. goes road runner to "Roadrunner" to transnational road runner to world runner. Each one a version, a double and an opposite, each one an expansion of the last. I am not saying all of history leads up to this moment but I am not *not* saying that. Rich as "Roadrunner" is, it is not paid in full until the opening of "Bamboo Banga," having completed the unfolding that leads from the hermetic idyll of a suburban teen to the global order of things. But we are coming to suspect that the end was present in the beginning. A dialectic has to expand just like capital.

It is easy to miss the fact that "Bamboo Banga" is also hilarious, M.I.A. is "hungry like the wolves hunting dinner dinner," and instantly we remember Duran Duran, their sublime song practically canceled out by its awful video, an orientalist vision it barely bothers to ironize, the beautiful pale boys in their South

Asian fantasia, their lead singer at the climax grappling on the jungle floor with a woman no doubt meant to be "native." Native to where? The video clip was shot in, yes, Sri Lanka, and we can see that "Bamboo Banga" means to be the exact inverse of world picture offered in "Hungry Like the Wolf," means to be the colonial travelogue but seen from the perspective of the colonized. She's banging on the door of your Hummer Hummer. The world town is coming for Simon Le Bon. At least Simon says, near the end of the song, "Strut on the line, it's discord and rhyme," which must be his verdict on the aesthetics of new wave but really this sounds about right for M.I.A., discord and rhyme pushed to their limits. By now the links are coming hot and fast, you start to wonder if you are suffering from a tendency to discover patterns where there are none, *apophenia*, they call it, or maybe it is the not you but the artist herself who suffers from such a malady, but isn't the name Duran Duran originally from that movie *Barbarella*, the one where the tousle-headed adventurer is drawn into a civil war and transforms into a 50 Foot Terrorist? And it isn't ten seconds before M.I.A. arrives at the rhyme for "dinner dinner" and it's "Barbarella look like she my dead ringer" as if to make sure *we* know *she* knows, knows she is riding this incredibly elaborate circuit, and she says "I'm a Roadrunner, a *world* runner" just to clarify things, she is in your system and she is trying to *become* the system like Wintermute at the end of *Neuromancer* except it's not the future it's now, represent now world town, and already she has said "Now I'm *sitting* down *chillin*' on *gun* powder" and then comes the internal rhyme we have been awaiting without quite knowing it since her first single, "*strike* match *light* fire, *who's* that girl *called* Maya?" and then the answer, the promise, the closing of the sonic loop: "M.I.A. coming back with *power power*." It's not quite a refrain, closer to the chant that is her nearest approach to an orienting form, Double Dutch again, martial and menacing and exultant. For the most part, the songs in this period evade conventional Western song structure and that is part of their power power. It's the other side of "Road-runner," which lacks a conventional song form because in a profound sense nothing can happen, that is the magic of the night. In these M.I.A. songs anything can happen, and that as we know is the heart of terror.

At the time people liked to worry about whether or not M.I.A. advocated political violence, whether that is okay, whether she had a right or a capacity to do so in any real way. It's not a new question. Maybe it is one of the oldest questions about art, one that has never been resolved. It comes up a lot in the seventies, near the peak of British punk's insurrectionary fervor and the anxious liberal reaction that follows, and one acerbic tune says "Mix me a molotov, I'm on the headline" before declaiming, "wanna be a gunslinger, don't be a rock singer" and heading for the chorus, "talk about … pop muzik." Same song from near where we started, we have come 'round again. It is easy to accuse M.I.A. of *radical chic* and many critics have. It is easy but maybe we want to stipulate that radical chic is among other things just the name

for how figural militancy exchanged for cash is never actual freedom struggle, like, no shit, and we might also want to stipulate
that the fetishizing of Third World militancy doesn't begin with
brown people, and while we're at it we might want to stipulate
that the burden of being consigned to appear rather than to act,
and the fate of being rewarded and blamed for appearance, falls
most heavily on women. Okay that was a lot of stipulating, but,
one more, let's stipulate that, sure, this music is indeed radical
chic. That too is a living tradition and one that is about as capable
of being great as anything else, don't act like you've never heard
the Clash.

The Clash are a useful comparison, another London band and
maybe the only one that can keep up with M.I.A. even if they're a
bit more provincial. Joe Strummer called his music "the sound of
the Westway," that concrete swoop built to be part of Ringway 1, a
project blocked by community protest and never completed. The
ghost of a ring road. Strummer would peer down at the cars on
the flyway from the window of Mick Jones's tower block flat and
memorialize the road in "London's Burning," everyone a roadrunner, everywhere that highway sound, "Up and down the Westway,
in and out the lights, what a great traffic system, it's so bright. I
can't think of a better way to spend the night, than speeding
around underneath the yellow lights." This is Richman's practically spiritual sense that nothing can happen out there, returned
as proto-revolutionary: "London's burning with boredom now!"

The Clash have a songwriting credit on the penultimate track of *Kala*, "Paper Planes," which samples their song "Straight to Hell" and goes straight to work, it builds a chorus from children singing "All I wanna do is . . ." and then the instantly familiar hook formed entirely of sound effects, the gunshots from the end of "World Town" coming back around, four of them and a rifle chambering a round, followed by an analog cash register chiming like a bell, some things are inevitable. *Bang-bang-bang-bang, click, ch-ching*. It's a first-person shooter except more properly it's a first-person vendor, a drug-dealing narrator in whom guns and money come together, *click, ch-ching*. The video clip, shot in the diasporic communities of Bed-Stuy in Brooklyn, is all about that mercantile life, buying and selling food, drugs, jewelry in the informal markets of the informalized. Obsessive shots of bills, what hip-hop for a while called *paper*, alternate with shots showing paper planes winging through New York, composed to make sure we get the wordplay in the title. *I shall show you a god-damned objective correlative*, the song says, money on the wing, capital flight, diaspora of dollars, the entire logic of circulation distilled down to a single dream image. The song is nothing if not the summary statement on global circulation, beginning right in the thick of it: "I fly like paper, get high like planes, if you catch me at the border I got visas in my name."

It is a great song and she knows it. When she sings, "No one on the corner got swagger like us," it is another hip-hop formula about slanging dope but also a true account of the music. We believe her. She's a world runner and for a moment she seems to run the world. But the song escapes the taut fabric of the album, in part by having something like a conventional chorus, a hook, a catchy melody, the kinds of things her music has for the most part avoided. So of course it is her biggest hit. "Paper Planes" is released as a single on August 23, 2008. It gets sampled immediately for "Swagga Like Us," by T.I., Kanye West, Jay-Z, Lil Wayne, and M.I.A. herself. Events are moving swiftly. Summer turns to fall. On September 27, 2008, "Swagga Like Us" reaches number 5 on the Hot 100, and "Paper Planes" sits at number 4. The M.I.A. era peaks and exhausts itself. In the brief interim between the single's release date and its seizure of the Top 10, Lehman Brothers folds with more than $600 billion in assets, the largest bankruptcy in history, making Long-Term Capital Management's failure exactly a decade earlier seem like a dress rehearsal in a dollhouse. The register chimes in "Paper Planes" take on a special resonance, maybe the gun shots too. *Bang-bang-bang-bang, click, ch-ching,* it's murder on the trading floor. The deeply correlated financial system, the one that is everywhere and nowhere with headquarters in New York and London, races to the edge of the precipice, past it, floats on nothing. But it is not just abstract finance that tanks, a world unto itself. There can no longer be any worlds unto themselves. The bubble was built in the first place because an economy no longer able to sustain itself making, you know, *cars* and the like—not that we should be nostalgic for the old economy, its own tribulation—made instead a series of bubbles and the last one was blown from sketchy mortgages foisted on desperate people who would shortly be pushed out of their homes in the cruel end game of financial scheming, let's call it radical chicanery.

How do we name this span of years, "Galang" to "Paper Planes," a span that is also the one in which the valuation of Gilead Sciences lifts into the empyrean, the one in which suicide bombing increases globally by an order of magnitude? Not identical periods but close enough, a brief passage of time wherein the artist comes as close to reality as art can get without imploding. It may be relatively simple. The M.I.A. era opens with the War on Terror and closes with systemic financial collapse. One of those things is laughably misnamed and one is not. Matters no doubt look different from different places, though that truth is only half of the mystery sometimes called *combined and uneven development* and sometimes just called the world as it goes: that because of ongoing asymmetrical warfare at a planetary scale, a war conducted with greenbacks and fighter jets, paper and planes, because of this events emanating outward from the imperial centers must not just *appear* but *be* everywhere. This is just another way of saying what it means that the breadth of the world has been drawn into a single great circuit, one but unequal.

M.I.A. is perfect for this, alas. It is a drastic fate, child of empire, child of diaspora, child of terror. Terror that always begins with the imperium and in a cruel deceit becomes the name for fighting back. If she had not existed, history would have had to invent her, its very own Electro Barbarella, just to narrate this period. She is the unity of the two events, War on Terror and economic collapse, she bridges them, you could say she holds them together. But they were always entangled, both of them inextricable from the events with which we started, the rise of U.S. industrial production with empire following, and then eventually unraveling. We come in near the end. For a while across the twentieth century, the United States maintains its centrality because the nations that play along make bank by doing so, they grab a share of the profits that flow toward the center, but when that current dries up, it is down to military arms. That is to say, financial collapse, and the intractable economic decline that it rode in on, do not end the unendable metawar—but they do manage to expose it for the murderous hoax that it always was: not a war on terror but a last-ditch effort to impose by main force another American Century, not particularly New, just one single catastrophe that keeps piling wreckage upon wreckage. And so it is that the factories of Lowell end in the bombing of Afghanistan and the foreclosure of nine million homes.

But that is to see things from the perspective of the United States, and though one cannot escape such a view because it is an artifact of power and power cannot be wished away, one must not stop there. For one thing, M.I.A. is not formed in America, though eventually she will relocate there, marry a billionaire, divorce him in relatively short order, the pop star usual. But it is never as simple as just saying where the artist is from. The hope is not to find the right place in particular. There is no single place, finally; the songs are trying to see matters from the standpoint of the world, they say so over and over. This is exactly the thing that M.I.A. is trying to grasp, the representational problem for pop music, pop music that is not *in* London, Paris, New York, Munich any more than bird flu is *in* Hong Kong or Guangdong, economic contagion is *in* Thailand or Brazil, terrorism is *in* Beirut or Colombo or Charlottesville. All of these things are in a situation, all of these things have conditions of possibility and they are the same conditions, and the structures that carry pop music carry the others as well, they are riders in the space of flows that was built by people, in history, the great ring road that we built for reasons that profit some and not others, that delivers life here for death elsewhere, all of these things are Roadrunners and it is very hard to say where they come from or where they are going, and the paper and the planes go around and around.

06 In Love with the Modern World, 1972

"IT ALL BEGINS WHERE IT ENDS," that is the rule of the ring road. So sang Roxette in 1989, in a song inevitably called "Joyride." Even they figured it out and they're from Sweden. And so we end at the beginning, with the ur-story.

Here is Jonathan Richman, incomparably in love with music, immediately adjacent to the radio—and out on the ring road he encounters not just one but a series of ordinary objects, commodities and their remnants, he's got the power of the AM, the factories and the auto signs, and he recognizes where another might not their beauty, discovers the absolute extraordinariness of the ordinary, and he is so moved by this that knows he must deliver this message and so, tears in his eyes, he begins to sing.

It is a story not of apophenia but epiphany, its opposite and other. Rather than discovering patterns where there are none, it is the revelation of the world's unity, though this modern epiphany is not the manifestation of Christ who haunts Route 128 as an absence where indigenous people once made kin. Instead it is the unity of the made world, the cars on the ring road, the songs on the radio, and the neon when it's cold outside.

The song is about the revelation of this unity and it is also the unity itself. Not just "Roadrunner" but each of our songs contains a song within it, narrates its own coming into being, how it arises from that highway sound, from all the songs on the radio, songs on the turntable, on the film soundtrack, and how it arises just the same from the real conditions that surround it in their ceaseless transformations. The moment beneath the modern moonlight in which Jonathan begins to sing, in which the song becomes itself.

But we have not stayed in the following moment with the patience it deserves. Or we have leapt too swiftly from Jonathan in his car to the song in the world, from *radio on* to *on the radio*, to the song as a thing in the world and its precursors and its afterlives and now, when everything is at an end, I want to go back again and this time stay with Jonathan for a moment longer.

Though he is not much of a singer he begins to sing. We have taken his feelings to be a kind of solitary elation, caught in the grip of epiphany. But something about epiphany is intolerable. If this is when "Roadrunner" truly begins it is also the moment at which it ends, or begins to end, somewhere within the song's great momentum, its endless turn, somewhere we can't quite pinpoint, the moment when the song that at first exists as a way to be with all songs, that at first exists for a teenager alone in the dark, is given over to the world.

Though he is not much of a singer he begins to sing and what happens when he does this? He makes the slightest shift, almost imperceptible, and then he is no longer *adjacent to* but *inside* the radio glowing there just within reach, he enters into the paradise of the dashboard lights, that becomes his future. He is now the author of the letter that someone will hear coming out of the darkness, out of the radio, the message that we will one day receive, he will now be the song heard by me and you and Tjinder Singh and Maya Arulpragasam just as theirs will be the songs heard by the next listener, the next driver, the next runner out there on the ring road. This is ecstasy the way the classical Greeks meant it, *ekstasis*, literally out of place, beside yourself. The pop single traffics ceaselessly in this ecstasy. That is its claim on the spiritual: how it lifts you out of yourself, how you feel in touch with something larger, maybe it is all the other listeners in the dark, maybe it is the everything.

Though he is not much of a singer, he begins to sing, sings where he had previously been a listener, and if the song is a record of inhabiting this moment as fully as it has ever been inhabited, it is also the moment from which Jonathan withdraws, the moment he begins to turn away from the greatest American rock song of the era and everything that it knows. From what does he withdraw? That is the mystery waiting at the end of all the other mysteries.

Though the singer does not always know everything the song knows, what circulates through the song, what the song circulates, perhaps this time he has a feel for the larger sense of an ending of which the song is all too aware, just as the song knows that the beauty Jonathan experiences as his own is not destined to last. The unity that is revealed to him is in every regard real but it is doomed. Not doomed in that manner borrowed from the most tedious poetry, larded with stuff that white guys figured out they could feel marketably tragic about, trade name "finitude," childhood ends, everybody dies, etc. Instead it is an identification with history itself, with its ebb and flow, its dark and ceaseless motion just out of reach, an identification with place and time as their axes intersect and in so doing place all of us in their crosshairs, all of this is why we began with an insistence on *American* and *era*, the spirit of 1972 patient on the ring road next to '73, the collapse of manufacturing and industrial profits, the tilt from Boom to Bust, ruination for the postwar compact of Bretton Woods, oil shock and oil crisis, stagflation, the hollowing of the labor movement, final humiliation in Vietnam, and on and on, causes and effects purling together until nobody can tell one from the other and it all goes ambient, becomes an atmosphere, the sense that a very particular arrangement that we have all agreed to call for lack of a better term *the modern world* is coming undone. He realizes his love for this world at exactly the moment of its ending, this is what illuminates the moment like neon from the inside, how that beauty is not separate from a world's unraveling, the peak and decline of Fordism, the peak and decline of the American century, the peak and decline of rock & roll.

Or perhaps he suffers from the anxiety of the modern, that we might vanish inside our machines, inside the media that we have made, the youngest daughter lost within the television in *Poltergeist*, the abusive neighbor boy captured inside the radio in Helen Reddy's "Angie Baby."

Or perhaps it is less metaphysical than all that, lodged instead within the transformation from listener to performer that happens when Jonathan though he is not much of a singer begins to sing, the little leap from consumer to producer. It is a leap whose immediacy has been greatly valued by, especially, punk and hip-hop, here's three chords, here is a turntable, now you're the band—driven by the dream of bypassing expertise, professionalism, the expensive lessons and pricey gear of the aesthetic classes. You just go directly from the audience to the stage, from the car to the car radio.

The ur-story is among other things a meditation on this experience or desire, a way to linger in the midst of the leap, to make the moment last. "Song of the Kite" is perhaps the crudest example which is why we started there. Because that song is untrusting it is burdened with Christian imagery so you will understand that this is a *revelation*, get it? But its insight is to choose the figure of the radio disc jockey, for is not the DJ a fantastical figuration of this whole idea, of being midleap, simultaneously *radio on* and *on the radio*, crouched there among piles of records? A lover of music so profoundly that this has become a profession, but still not an artist, not quite; simultaneously both listener and performer, receiver and transmitter; between the music of others and their own music yet to come, there in the glow of the studio lights. "Kite" is entirely about this pause between two worlds, so that we can experience the leap, the revelation usually confined to a burning instant, as a sustained experience unfolding over time. What happens after is hazy, maybe someday your name will be in lights, it's left to the future. The thing happens, and that is enough.

Or it is supposed to be. But it is from this that Jonathan withdraws, right in the middle of the song. He does not want to make the leap. He's got the radio on and he likes it that way, he does not want to disappear into it. This is why there can be no chorus, no hook, those are the sorts of deliverables you provide once the leap is complete and you are a pop star. They are what the future sounds like when your name is definitely in lights. Instead, not long after turning the song over to the band, he says, "Alright! Bye-bye!" and he drives away from us, drives away from the song, drives away from the transformation that the song puts on offer, but, joke's on him, he's on a ring road and we know he will come back around, play the song one more time. We are forever coming back to "Roadrunner" just as we are forever leaving it behind, and is this not also Jonathan's story, the recursive and impossible renunciation of the song, the sound, the moment, the labels and contracts, the recording sessions, the life he could have had?

The Modern Lovers who first record "Roadrunner" in 1972 fragment two years later, but the name survives for a while, "what he's always called whatever band he's played with," until finally abandoned in the late eighties.[1] Ernie Brooks works with a series of more and less avant-garde musicians, Jerry Harrison joins Talking Heads, David Robinson leaves, comes back again, finally decamps for another band out of Boston that he names the Cars, whose biggest international hit will be called "Drive." Robinson's last recording with Modern Lovers is the 1976 album that Richman insists—contra the assembled demos that form *The Modern Lovers*, also released that year—is the band's real debut, *Jonathan Richman and the Modern Lovers*. The latter album does not include "Roadrunner" but it does feature, as if you could somehow escape your fate by throwing the car into reverse, a cover of "Back in the U.S.A." It is the bicentennial of the nation founded on the lash, the land grab, and the Lowell System, but it is also exactly two decades since 1956 patient in the bushes, now that is a goddamned phenomenology of spirit. "Did I miss the skyscrapers," Jonathan asks, holding onto Berry's syllables too avidly and falling off the rhythm like an awkward kid, missing a word or two, ". . . and the long freeways?" That highway sound, that nation sound.

People see the renunciation of "Roadrunner" as a break and it is told that way, not least by Richman himself. The comic 1991 track "Monologue About Bermuda," an elaborated version of the earlier "Down in Bermuda," recounts the band's 1973 residency at the Inverurie Hotel, where Jonathan concludes that his earlier material is stiff at best and maybe something worse, and turns to the gentler, sweeter sound that he will carry forward all the way into this book's present. That is the first break but not the last, maybe it begins with leaving Los Angeles with that first album incomplete, maybe it culminates with moving to the Sierra foothills near the millennium, and then there is the time around 1980 when he sojourns for a couple years in Appleton, Maine, playing local bars like Barbara's Place in nearby Belfast, located in a former Chevy dealership because history is horrible but it is shapely.[2]

The withdrawal, the renunciation, the break, it is all of it inarguable. But there is a way to honor that tale and at the same time discover within it its own opposite, a continuity of such care and depth that it has gone almost unseen. Suppose one sped forward across break after break, left "Roadrunner" to the rearview, left it belonging to everyone and no one like a true folktale, and chose one seemingly tossed-off song from among dozens, hundreds that fill the years, let's say the track called "Chewing Gum Wrapper." It is from 1985's *Rockin' & Romance* and it is about exactly what its title promises, he is walking along one day and spots the "cruddy little chewing gum wrapper" discarded on the ground, about which his verdict is, "I love the faded colors like what end up at the dump, my heart go bumpety, bumpety, bumpety-bump." It is a relatively conventional song, choruses following verses with a bridge in the middle, he recounts this encounter several times without much changing, the song goes nowhere. That is all that happens, nothing more, nothing less.

We could not claim this is a version of the ur-story. Too many elements are missing. He has lost the car and misplaced the road, forgotten the radio, abandoned any concern with the modern world. The encounter lacks the force of revelation that might transform him. In fact everything is missing except one feature: the abject and trivial object that is encountered alone but still shimmers with unity, with secret relation. "Cruddy little chewing gum wrapper dried up by the sun," he sings, "someone else got to feel this way because I can't be the only one." There it is, the spectral presence of the everyone in the least thing. That single element is strangely insistent, or maybe it is his delight in such an object and in its revealed beauty that insists across a dozen years and more, insists on continuity with the Jonathan curving along Route 128 in and around 1972.

The object, that is to say, is popular in the sense offered at the outset, as in *barrio popular* or *quartier populaire*, where the common people live, the places that are always being torn up to make way for "progress." Popular as in the mass-market commodity, what is left of the popular in a world where people are forced to buy what they need to survive, a world where everything has become a commodity and stop pretending it hasn't, don't be a hippie. The chewing gum wrapper, the abject and trivial thing, is popular and also it is trash, its usefulness extinguished, now freed to be perfectly beautiful. Obviously—by which I don't mean to diminish the object or its significance, it's just that we have been together for twenty-nine thousand words and certain things have come clear—obviously if we follow this genre of object back to its source it is the pop song, the radio single, used up and faded and corroded and still beautiful, the pop song to which you listen alone in your car, your bedroom, and in your solitude you are with all the other listeners, *someone else got to feel this way*. "It helps me from being alone," he sang once upon a time in "Twice." And obviously the always-new delight of the always-old object is the pleasure of the pop song that even in its exhaustion is inexhaustible, finally without end, still a revelation, bumpety, bumpety, bumpety-bump.

But there is more to say about the chewing gum wrapper on the pavement, magnificently itself and also stand-in for the radio single, more to say about its trampled beauty, its proletarian spirit, its quality as remnant and refuse, not even the chewing gum but its wrapper, not even the wrapper but its wreckage, no longer wrapping anything, the gum itself long since masticated and abandoned to its true fate of forming an infinitesimal fraction of the planet's mantle. I do not mean to rehearse the familiar celebration of the virtues of uselessness, of waste and excess, regularly proffered on art's behalf as a remedy for, or subversion of, the world that wants everything to be useful, instrumental, profitable. Rather, all of this is to note the pointed but entirely unmarked separation between the object in question and the necessary moment of its making: the fabrication of the gum, the wrapper, the machine that makes each, the machine that wraps one in the other. All of these processes required someone to do the work. Each of them is a job. And that is the final which is to say the first secret of circulation, gestured toward earlier, how it cannot be disentangled from the production whose existence it always disguises; how once released into the market, into the world of exchange and the great circulation, the common object points always toward and always away from the work of forcing it into being.

While it may not immediately appear so, it is the very same problem that we encountered first in Chuck Berry, a problem, that is to say, entangled with the birth of the genre. This is the division that appears at first, and in the commonplaces of cultural lore, to map directly onto that between teen and adult, innocence and experience, country boy and city lights, but is finally something else, intimately related, absolutely distinct: the fantastical separation of *no particular place to go* from the call to order, the division of the ring road from *ring! ring! goes the bell*. Rock & roll is premised on the separation of the joyride from the factory.

In lingering with a four-minute song about driving around at night listening to the radio, this may seem an arbitrary and abstruse place to end, and yet that is where the song begins, in this exact separation. Jonathan is flying into the world and he recognizes his situation, that is what revelation is after all, it is just a recognition accelerated to faster miles an hour. Though he is not much of a singer, he begins to sing, he sings the world of commodities and their remnants, the entire set of sublunary things that will provision "Roadrunner," but like all recognitions, this one is two-sided and even while flying into it he begins to withdraw, not from the beauty, not from the unity, but from the accompanying leap. He encounters before him the made world— but—*the made world without its makers*, just Jonathan and a road, a suburb, a state, a civilization spread out beneath the moonlight in which he might endlessly list the built, the fabricated, the pre- recorded, the artifacts of an otherwise absent race that spangle the landscape through which he rides, the only person alive until that startling turn three minutes into "Twice" when he politely requests, "OK now you say it Modern Lovers" and we discover with a start that he is not alone in the car, and they sing, "RADIO ON" to start the call-and-response outro, but it is already too late, already the other side of the ecstasy has been thrown into stark relief, what it means and what it entails, and he does not want to stop being a teenager in love with the modern world and dis- appear into the radio, disappear into work and professionalism, disappear into production.

And is that not the utopian problem of the ur-story? The leap that it contemplates, thematizes, sustains, is the moment in which the separation is overcome and the unity that feels holy

is revealed as the simple truth that someone works at the Stop &
Shops and the factories, someone works at the recording studios
and the record stores. All different, all the same; if he makes the
leap then he will slot in there somewhere. The utopian problem is
not how to slot into the right place, as the rock & roll star, but how
not to do it, how not to disappear. From this everything follows.

He is the most amateur of amateurs, every break and withdrawal was to preserve some fraction of this, he blew up the
contract to stay an amateur even after he started recording the
record, he blew up the band, started over and over, ended over
and over, he did whatever he could to stay adjacent to the radio
without ever quite disappearing into it. Maybe someday his name
would be in lights, nah, maybe not.

We could argue quite reasonably that his revelation takes
this form rather than the one that captured Chuck Berry, *radio
on* rather than *on the radio*, in no small part because for all the
repetitions of the ring road, the echoes and recurrences we have
watched go past, their moments are different. Jonathan sets out
on his neon circumnavigation not at the heights of the Long
Boom but at its end as, beyond the edges of the scene, the great
engine of expansion that bore aloft rock & roll and much else
reaches the limits of its mad ascent and begins to ride on down-
ward to darkness.

It is a commonplace that, inquiring after historical truth, we
arrive always too early or too late. "Roadrunner" arrives mirac-
ulously on time, nosing out onto the Great Circulator at the

very moment that circulation, forever reaching outward from the centers of production to draw the wide vistas of the continent into the fatal form of the nation, takes on the gleam of a new necessity, which is to say, desperation. But the song holds on to the pleasure of its own timeliness, of inhabiting this transformation entirely, this moment of perfect balance, a night built from music and flickering signs, hypnotic thrum underneath, no other humans around to break the spell, it's like discovering, without quite noticing when the change happened, that you are on another plane of existence, really it is just like driving through the radio itself, airwaves as landscape: song advertisement song song advertisement whirring past. It is *like* that but not quite. The song will not give in to the abstraction, it holds tight to physical speed, faster miles an hour, that highway sound, this is as close to disappearing into the radio as Jonathan is willing to get, perfect really. Out on Route 128 he can feel the end of things where once was the power and the glory, and this perhaps is what gives the song its full weight, how the car and the night and the radio are charged with the innocence of 1955 and the melancholy of 1972 both, the former forever folded into and cached inside the latter, like all good stories this one carries within it its opposite, they are for a moment the same, rise and fall in two simple chords.

What is the third term, then: rise, fall, ——? The song doesn't know, is not obliged to know. No moment knows all the others, no four minutes know all of time. Even at its wild velocity it does not get ahead of itself. From the promontory of the present we know a bit more about the song's future, its persistence and trans-formation, the way that just as 1955 is folded and cached inside 1972, 1972 will be in turn folded and cached inside 1997, 1997 folded and cached inside 2007, 2007 folded and cached inside right now, the moonlight always modern, the moonlight never modern, each year containing within it those that came before, each song passing along the roadside the spirit of some previous moment that feels originary, and only through the presence of the past is the future open.

This is not to suggest therefore some sort of eternal return, one catastrophe forever on repeat. The circuit keeps expanding, pushing up against the limits of genre, nation, world-system. The new happens. When we come back around again we are still connected to where we started, the red thread wound into a spool—no, not a spool but a spiral, we are changed as the world is changed. Always that uncanny identity of continuity and break for which the spiral is the true figure, stamped right there on the vinyl.

Now, when everything is at an end, give me your hand, so that we may begin again from the beginning, that is my favor-ite sentence by my favorite thinker and the logic of it is pure ring road, pure *play that song one more time*, but we understand that when we come around again things must be different, must be changed enough that we have a chance to get it right this time, this is the meaning of revolution, right, bye-bye.

ACKNOWLEDGMENTS

I am first and foremost indebted to the music and the musicians: Chuck Berry, Private Lightning, Tjinder Singh and Cornershop, M.I.A., and especially Jonathan Richman and the Modern Lovers. But also all the others who may appear here peripherally but are near the center of other stories.

This book began as a twenty-minute talk that would later be published in *Best American Music Writing*; I am grateful to the editors, Greil Marcus and Daphne Carr. That talk was first presented at the annual pop conference in Seattle, and much of my gratitude lies there, starting with Ann Powers and Eric Weisbard—both for their efforts on behalf of the music-writing world and for their longtime kindness to me. Over the years, I have met many people at the conference who have challenged and changed my thinking, including my coeditor for this series, the brilliant Emily Lordi. I met Ken Wissoker at the very first PopCon and we argued about Adorno; I forget who took what position but he was probably right. I would like to thank him as well as everyone else at Duke University Press for their support. An index seems like a kindness scholars offer each other but in truth it is a skilled labor done often by another scholar and always in hurried circumstances; thanks to Kurt Newman for this one.

I am grateful for the ongoing friendship of Stephen Smith, who carries Boston rock with him wherever he goes. This book in many ways has its origins with him and with everyone else who worked at that restaurant in Coolidge Corner to pay for their music habit, especially friends who were or would be in Salem 66, Throwing Muses, and Hole. Damon Krukowski, speaking of Boston rock, has been an ongoing source of musical knowledge. Anahid Nersessian provided valuable insights and invaluable encouragement during the writing of this book. I wrote a lot of it sitting with Juliana Spahr, beloved friend and writing partner. It is important to say that seemingly individual works are always expressions of collective experience and thought, and my collective starts with Chris Nealon, who has been my cothinker of music and social relations since we met (though all failings herein are entirely my own). I would also like to thank Greta Kaplan, with whom I shared vinyl; Carol Clover, who is the most musical person I know; and finally Seeta Chaganti, an unparalleled model for thinking carefully and deeply about art, artifice, and artifacts—and who also saw me through death and back during the writing of this book. It is for her.

Writing a book about one song is painful because you have to choose the song, and that means forsaking the other songs you wanted to write a book about, the other singles that you almost chose, that feel both immediate and like they have the infinite within them—which, for the record, were "Tell Me Something Good," "Jolene," "Dim All the Lights," "Freedom '90," and Fuck the Police.

NOTES

Chapter 1. Rock & Roll Radio, 1980

1. Canetti, *Crowds and Power*, 155.

Chapter 2. Faster Miles an Hour, 1972

1. Mitchell, *There's Something about Jonathan*, 20.
2. Vasari, *Lives of the Artists*, 177.
3. Mitchell, *There's Something about Jonathan*, 20.
4. Marcus, *Lipstick Traces*, 60.
5. Ross, *Fast Cars, Clean Bodies*, 21.
6. Stop & Shop, "Our History."
7. Mitchell, *There's Something about Jonathan*, 20.
8. Lees-Maffei, "Men, Motors, Markets and Women," 363.
9. Stephen Bayley quoted in Lees-Maffei, "Men, Motors, Markets and Women," 368.
10. Sagan, *Aimez-vous Brahms*, 11.
11. Benjamin, *Illuminations*, 222.

Chapter 3. That Highway Sound, 1955

1. Barton, "The Car, the Radio, the Night."
2. Christgau, *Any Old Way You Choose It*, 144.
3. Powers, "Bittersweet Little Rock and Roller."
4. Walsh, *Astral Weeks*, 120.
5. Hans Thomalla, personal correspondence, April 4, 2017.
6. McNeil, "Modern Lovers Bassist Ernie Brooks."
7. L. Robinson, "New Velvet Underground," 90.
8. Quoted in Mitchell, *There's Something about Jonathan*, 72–73.
9. Ross, *Fast Cars, Clean Bodies*, 19.
10. Smucker, *Why the Beach Boys Matter*, 16.
11. Christgau, "Ain't That a Shame."
12. Mitchell, *There's Something about Jonathan*, 26.
13. Smucker, *Why the Beach Boys Matter*, 21.
14. Ross, *Fast Cars, Clean Bodies*, 39.
15. Flink, *Car Culture*, 211.

Chapter 4. The Main Streets and the Cinema Aisles, 1997

1. Eliot, "London Letter," 510.
2. Ganti, *Producing Bollywood*, 78–79.
3. Ganti, *Producing Bollywood*, 42.
4. Ganti, *Producing Bollywood*, 75.
5. Ganti, *Producing Bollywood*, 33–34.
6. Quoted in Hyder, *Brimful of Asia*, 151.

Chapter 5. World Runner, 2007

1. Arulpragasam, *M.I.A.*, n.p.
2. Quoted in Lynskey, "Fighting Talk."
3. Pape, "Tamil Tigers."
4. Davis, *Monster at Our Door*, 8,
5. Davis, *Monster at Our Door*, 56.
6. J. Robinson, *Economic Philosophy*, 45.
7. Davis, *Monster at Our Door*, 69.
8. Davis, *Monster at Our Door*, 83.
9. Abrams et al., "PNAC—Statement of Principles."

Chapter 6. In Love with the Modern World, 1972

1. Marcus, *Lipstick Traces*, 61.
2. This detail is drawn from the remarkable excavation of this period by Roiland, "Something Like Springtime."

BIBLIOGRAPHY

Abrams, Elliot, Gary Bauer, William J. Bennett, Jeb Bush, Dick Cheney, Eliot A. Cohen, Midge Decter, et al. "PNAC—Statement of Principles." June 3, 1997. https://www.rrojasdatabank.info/pfpc/PNAC---statement%20of%20principles.pdf.

Arulpragasam, Maya. *M.I.A.* London: Pocko, 2002.

Barton, Laura. "The Car, the Radio, the Night—And Rock's Most Thrilling Song." *The Guardian*, July 20, 2007.

Benjamin, Walter. *Illuminations*. New York: Random House, 1986.

Canetti, Elias. *Crowds and Power*. Translated by Carol Stewart. New York: Continuum, 1973.

Christgau, Robert. "Ain't That a Shame." *Barnes and Noble Review*, September 6, 2010. https://www.barnesandnoble.com/review/aint-that-a-shame.

Christgau, Robert. *Any Old Way You Choose It: Rock and Other Pop Music, 1967–1973*. New York: Cooper Square Press, 2000.

Davis, Mike. *The Monster at Our Door: The Global Threat of Avian Flu*. New York: New Press, 2005.

Eliot, T. S. "London Letter." *The Dial* 72, no. 5 (May 1922): 510–13.

Flink, James J. *The Car Culture*. Cambridge, MA: MIT Press, 1975.

Ganti, Tejaswini. *Producing Bollywood*. Durham, NC: Duke University Press, 2012.

Hyder, Rehan. *Brimful of Asia: Negotiating Ethnicity in the UK Music Scene*. Aldershot, UK: Ashgate, 2004.

Lees-Maffei, Grace. "Men, Motors, Markets and Women." In *Autopia: Cars and Culture*, edited by Peter Wollen and Joe Kerr, 363–70. London: Phaidon, 2002.

Lynskey, Dorian. "Fighting Talk." *The Guardian*, April 21, 2005.

Marcus, Greil. *Lipstick Traces: A Secret History of the Twentieth Century*. Cambridge, MA: Harvard University Press, 1990.

McNeil, Legs. "Modern Lovers Bassist Ernie Brooks on Recording Their Classic Album." Please Kill Me, October 10, 2017. https://pleasekillme.com/modern-lovers-bassist-ernie-brooks/.

Mitchell, Tim. *There's Something about Jonathan: Jonathan Richman and the Modern Lovers*. London: Owen, 1997.

Pape, Robert. "Tamil Tigers: Suicide Bombing Innovators." *Talk of the Nation*, National Public Radio, May 21, 2009. https://www.npr.org/templates/story/story.php?storyId=104391493.

Powers, Ann. "Bittersweet Little Rock and Roller." *The Record*, National Public Radio, March 21, 2017. https://www.npr.org/sections/therecord/2017/03/21/520146232/bittersweet-little-rock-and-roller.

Robinson, Joan. *Economic Philosophy*. Abingdon, UK: Routledge, 2017.

Robinson, Lisa. "The New Velvet Underground." In *Rock She Wrote*, edited by Evelyn McDonnell and Ann Powers, 89 – 92. New York: Dell, 1995.

Roiland, Josh. "Something Like Springtime." *Popula*, November 11, 2018. https://popula.com/2018/11/11/something-like-springtime/.

Ross, Kristin. *Fast Cars, Clean Bodies: Decolonization and the Reordering of French Culture*. Cambridge, MA: MIT Press, 1995.

Sagan, Françoise. *Aimez-vous Brahms . . .* Translated by Peter Wiles. New York: Dutton, 1960.

Stop & Shop. "Our History." Accessed December 15, 2020. https://stopandshop.com/pages/about-us.

Smucker, Tom. *Why the Beach Boys Matter*. Austin: University of Texas Press, 2018.

Vasari, Giorgio. *The Lives of the Artists*. Oxford, UK: Oxford University Press, 2008.

Walsh, Ryan H. *Astral Weeks: A Secret History of 1968*. New York: Penguin, 2018.

INDEX